Child Abuse True Stories

by Ann Ford M.S.

Please see YETItips.com for the latest in practical self-help and abuse recovery books.

ISBN-13: 978-0-9840701-9-0

Contents

1 – CHILD ABUSERS ARE CRIMINALS   5

Victims no more – put the blame where it belongs - on the abusers   9

Seeing one's abusers punished   10

Ways some famous people have healed injuries   14

2 – ABOUT CHILD ABUSE AND NEGLECT   15

The U.S. leads the world in illegal drug use   16

Alcohol disordered adults abuse their kids 4 times more   17

What is neglect?   17

What is abuse?   18

What triggers adults to become violent in their abuse?   20

3 – WHAT'S BEHIND THE CRUELTY   22

Narcissistic Personality Disorder   25

When emotional drives turn to cruelty   26

FOUR DRIVES – some cause love, some cause cruelty   28

Abusing or neglecting children at home   29

When adult abuse of adult children is deliberate   31

Impact on adults from alcoholic and dysfunctional families   32

Substances and biology that cause brain problems   34

What alcoholics and other addicts are looking for   37

The influence an alcoholic has on a young victim   39

Watch out for the after-effects of being raised around alcoholics   40

4 – IT'S NOT YOUR FAULT - BE A SURVIVOR   43

Identify the trauma reaction style   45

Recovery options to be informed about   47

Take action to heal yourself – leave other people's problems alone   49

Family members may remain untrustworthy   50

Facets of forgiving - forgive to move forward   51

Assess your damage, then re-educate yourself to be a survivor   52

Physical, psychological, or sexual clues to abuse   54

Assessing the damage to you done by alcoholics or substance users   55

Invest in taking care of yourself   59

5 – TRUE STORIES OF CHILD ABUSE   61

    A way to know trauma occurred – look for traces of PTSD   62

6 – STEPS FOR HEALING   120

    Diagnosing the damage to plan a recovery   122

    Illnesses caused by neglect and abuse   123

    Avoid the old cast of characters   132

    Grieve the past and move on to joy   134

    Three aspects of grieving to consider   135

    Support options   136

    Every day increase your self validation   141

    Neglect or abuse is a part of your life journey   142

    Remember the "FACTS"   143

    Author's Bio   145

    Bibliography   146

    Index   147

1 – CHILD ABUSERS ARE CRIMINALS

"To have darkness behind me, in front of me a bright sky..."

Julia Hartwig

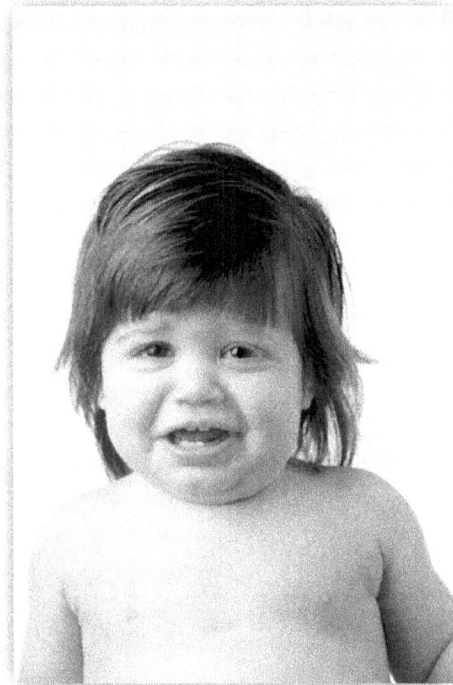

Causing ill treatment - abuse – of a child or person under the age of 18, is a crime in the U.S., with jail time. The laws are very recent, so many people are still used to child abuse. <u>Abusers are criminals</u>. They still abuse because they think no one will turn them in. Child abuse is power abuse.

The Penn State coach Sandusky intimidated victims into not reporting him. A former Mayor of Spokane, Washington who molested boys, and a former Mayor of Portland, Oregon, who molested a girl – each assumed no one would report them; they thought the POWER THEY HELD would protect them.

Child Abuse brings up a gigantic cultural conflict between children having the right to be safe, and abusive adults wanting to demonstrate their power. POWERFULNESS is a disparity in treatment – it IS unfair. The more someone wants to feel powerful over others, the more likely that they are to betray rules, laws at work, and ultimately LOVE within families – by abusing the easiest victims they can find – and kids are the "easiest" available victims.

Families have long concealed child abuse whenever the abuser had the "paycheck power", and for decades men made more money than women, so families didn't tell on male abusers. Families also used to be concerned with being "shamed" by these acts, with social "stigma".

Modern times have less shame attached to many acts, with nudity on television, and teenage pregnancies being prime-time entertainment. Women can now earn enough money that they don't have to stay with male abusers. In the U.S., shame and stigma are no longer as serious. And children are not seen as often as "property".

Celebrities are promoting organizations and "days" that draw attention to protecting kids, such as "Safe Kids Day." Actress Julia Roberts helps to promote awareness of the "Joyful Heart Foundation", which educates and empowers survivors of sexual assault, domestic violence and child abuse. Abusers are now very much more likely to experience the consequences their law-breaking actions deserve, including punitive financial damages and jail time.

Seeing that a craving for POWER is really behind these crimes, many police and U.S. district attorneys flex their own powerful "authority muscles", and relentlessly corner abusers, even when (1) the abusers are millionaires or rich, and (2) even when the abusers are being "protected" or "hidden" by others.

Some people ignore child abuse or neglect until they are "publicly outed" -

Most people don't even consider that multi-millionaires also contribute to child abuse – it seems unthinkable that someone who could solve a child neglect situation – could choose not to fix it. The singer Beyonce Knowles has a half brother – her 63 year old father Mathew Knowles was her manager until she fired him – and he sired a boy who is now 4-years old and homeless. Because Beyonce fired her father, he no longer pays any support of the child, who now lives in a homeless shelter. Could Beyonce share some of her millions and consider her 4-year old half-brother part of her world – instead of subjecting him to the trauma and neglect of being homeless? – certainly she could.

Some forms of child abuse are still treated as if they were irrelevant to the child – because other adults get distracted when the mentally ill parent goes so far out of the range of "normal behavior." People forget to factor in how profoundly harming the experience is to the child.

EXAMPLE:

A mother involved in her daughter's girl scout activities as a treasurer, stole $9,800 according to news sources, over a two-year period, which made the troop bankrupt and forced to disband. Darlene Jo Lewis used the money for gifts, to treat her son, and to buy herself the services of a dating service.

The impact on the little girl scout, is incalculable. She has been shamed in front of all of her friends – who will probably not be her friends anymore – and her mother is a criminal.

# # #

EXAMPLE:

In 2014, the television teen actress, 16-year old Ariel Winter, has been granted safety in the form of permanent custody, granted to her older sister Shanelle Gray, due to abuse at the hands of her mother.

# # #

EXAMPLE:

In March, 2014, news media reported that two elementary school girls who got in a fight on a school bus, ended up with their mothers committing crimes.

Both mothers arranged a "duel" with hand-guns, and one mother shot the other mother dead.

The murderer is being held without bond. One little girl is now orphaned.

# # #

Victims no more – put the blame where it belongs - on the abusers

The world dishes out tragedies of poor health and injuries to millions of people, and we are all truly brothers and sisters the world over, in having experienced some major injury or pain, growing up. The problem with deliberate child abuse is that the core of being alive for a child, is attacked: abuse is LOVE BETRAYAL; betrayal by a person that you trusted.

The sad legacy for many people who grow up **not** being allowed to talk about their abuse, is that they have **not** named the experience as neglect and abuse, and many *continue to falsely blame themselves*, because their abusers blamed them – the victims. Carrying the blame for the abusers, damages the children in that it BREAKS DOWN THEIR WILL – so that they have less willpower and confidence – and it makes it harder for them to recover.

Once the victim *speaks the truth* – that there is an abuser who is to blame – who is evading consequences – then a person can heal from almost 90% of the damage. The abusive injury is *not forgotten*, but it is no longer a self-destructive memory, because it can be counter-balanced by survivor behaviors. Survivors look out for themselves, and:

(1) Prevent future abuse.
(2) Avoid abusers from the past.
(3) It is urgent that former victims recognize that some people are jerks, or destructive, even if they are relatives, and should be avoided.
(4) You can't please everyone; some people are committed to being unhappy (it can be how they get attention), and you cannot make them happy no matter what you do.

There are many ways to measure healing progress, but one very simple way is to observe your efforts. "TAKE NO ACTION, SEE NO CHANGES. TAKE BIG ACTIONS – SEE BIG CHANGES." Have no fear taking action.

To be true to yourself you need to learn who you are, now, then you can take action.

> *"A shrinking violet learns to stand up for herself, she's not a shrinking violet anymore. When a thief quits stealing, he's no longer a thief,"*
>
> *Dr. Phil*

You have to take action. As actor Jon Hamm, recovering from alcohol abuse, and childhood abandonment, said: "It's much easier to participate in the reality you've created, rather than living in a world of regret."

Seeing one's abusers punished

When children (unlike adults) are neglected or abused, they are unskilled in absorbing the experience of betrayal of love, or the loss of love. Who you love – and whether they love your back – changes you. This can cause a wound for a person, that they carry into adulthood. The law, fortunately, frequently allows adults to go back and get financial damages from the abusers who abused them. This recognition and compensation can go a long way toward healing abuse wounds.

EXAMPLE:

An abuser who was "protected" was finally held to answer

One abuser was a principal, teacher, and coach, at 10 schools across the country. He spent 30 years being "protected" in the Catholic school system before he went into public schools, primarily in Washington and Nevada. What he typically did to his 50 Washington state victims, according to 2014 Seattle local news reports, was to rub himself on young boys until he experienced his own sexual release. He denied that (1) he was homosexual, (2) denied it was abuse, but was just "wrestling". Finally he was barred from being near students, and is responsible for <u>millions</u> of dollars of compensation paid to his abuse victims.

\# \# \#

Two young men who were sexually assaulted by Edward Courtney, using the initials "J.B.", and "D.C.", gave particularly specific accounts that nailed down the coffin on this child abuse monster. The satisfaction for these two articulate and brave men may be very high, and certainly they have earned the gratitude and admiration of all the other victims who needed such damning testimony to get Courtney out of schools. The victims all received financial settlements as well, which is another aspect of recovering from having been victimized – <u>the abuser must give the victim something back,</u> and <u>be punished</u>.

The Catholic church moved Edward Courtney around the country in various states, even with church administrators admitting in internal memos that he was a pedophile. The Catholic church paid for him to go to sexual abuse "rehab" counseling in Canada, multiple times, and finally paid the costs of getting him a college course that gave him a teaching certificate so he could teach in public schools. The church did not report him to the police, even though they were legally required to do so. The church gave him written letters of recommendation to public schools that were glowing, and false. Some of the former victims were able, despite the Catholic church's actions, to locate Edward Courtney and to have him prosecuted by U.S. District attorneys, and have the police put out a warrant for his arrest.

The Seattle Archdiocese has paid out over S50 million in recent years in settlements for sex assault lawsuits brought by 200 former students. The Catholic Christian Brothers had to declare bankruptcy in 2011, after paying $16.5 million to 400 former students. Of the 400 former students, 52 – 80 (some in the Chicago area), claimed Edward G. Courtney abused them.

EXAMPLE:

A wealthy child murderer was punished.

In 2014, Lindsey Lowe, a 20-year old who married a wealthy man, was carrying twin boys to term. As soon as they were born, at home, she smothered them and hid their bodies in the laundry room.

She is now serving two life sentences, for premeditated murder, and will not get out of jail until she is 77.

# # #

EXAMPLE:

A child abuser who was worth millions was caught and jailed

A Dallas, Texas socialite, living in a $1.4 million dollar home with her intellectual property attorney spouse, was a serial child abuser who distributed child pornography, for 12 years. Erica Susan Perdue is a 43-year old grandmother, who has been forced to pay restitution to one of the victims, as well as a $10,000 fine, and serve a 14-year jail sentence, and upon release complete 8 years of probation as a sex offender.

Undercover policemen tracked her downloading of child pornography, under her alias "classyb***h", and they arrested her in 2012. Her license plate was a vanity plate that read: "MY SYN".

# # #

As one assistant U.S. Attorney said, this person was an "unstable personality". She had her first child at 16, and had been divorced twice by her mid-twenties. Her mother, who insisted on anonymity, claimed that Erika had "Bi-polar Disorder".

It is comforting to know that despite stalling, all the legal protections she could afford, and using her large amount of wealth – this child abuser is behind bars.

Criminals in child abuse are being vigorously punished.

Ways some famous people have healed injuries

Children who have been abused and neglected _are not damaged goods_. King George of England was abused for several years by a nanny who pinched and slapped him and did not feed him, until finally by the age of four, his royal parents noticed that he had stomach problems. It took him decades working on the stuttering habit that resulted from all the fear and stress of his child abuse, but he finally conquered it with the bond of a best friend, his speech coach.

Oprah Winfrey overcame the lasting impact of her multiple experiences of sexual abuse, including a rape when she was a young teen – by eating to excess, then getting a grip on that eating over-consolation, and _by finding the ultimate consolation – telling the world the truth about child abuse_!

Another person who survived child abuse was Walt Disney, who overcame his feelings of hurt and resentment at being worked like a slave and beaten with a belt, by trying to _constantly summon up the positives in life, to counter-balance the darkness_.

These people lived lives that set examples of different ways to heal the injuries. Many, many millions of people have recovered from severe trauma and childhood abuse. Some have recovered through the act of defending others, until they realize they have made "events" as equal as can be. Some have gone through years of tears or soft tissue massage (done for torture victims to help recover, to dispel the fears that still are held hormonally in traumatized bodies.) Others have legally "stopped" abusers.

2 – ABOUT CHILD ABUSE AND NEGLECT

"No one was raised in Happyland. It doesn't exist."

Jon Hamm

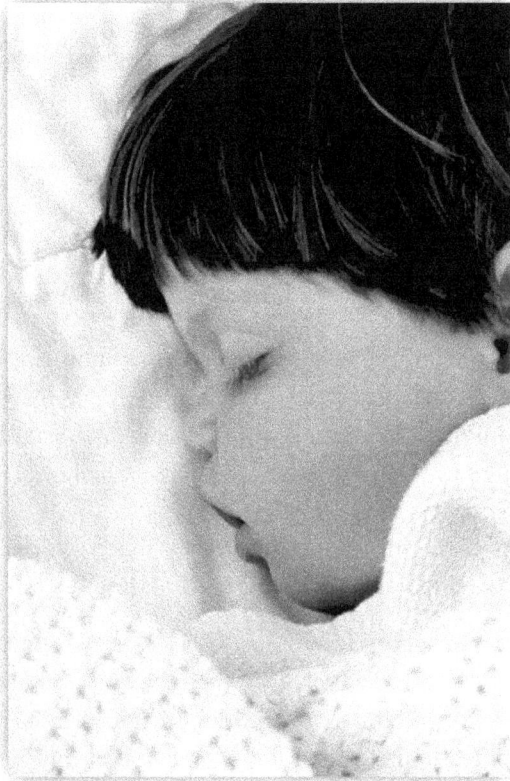

Every year more than 3 million reports of child abuse are made, that include 6 million children – and many incidents go unreported – and the numbers are increasing. Every day the U.S. has fatalities of between 4 to 7 children – that's children KILLED – from neglect and child abuse.

The Beth Israel Hospital chain reports that patient data shows that the majority of kids – more than 75% – grow up with some form of neglect, emotional abuse, sexual abuse or incest, or physical abuse. This is a national cultural crisis. Kids may be sitting in school being misdiagnosed with attention problems, when they are really exhausted and scared from being abused where they live, the night before.

These children lived through tragedies at ages too young to have the skills to INTEGRATE, MOURN, AND REBUILD their lives, after the injuries and neglect occurred. Children and teens are NOT adults and lack the experience and SKILLS needed to recover on their own.

The U.S. has one of the worst records of the industrialized countries in child abuse. The U.S. has a lot of parents who are addicts. More than 2/3 of most child abuse – and usually 80% of child sexual abuse – involves abusers using alcohol.

The U.S. leads the world in illegal drug use

An international survey found that the U.S. used 4 times more cocaine than any other country, and led the world in alcohol use – so for both legal and illegal drugs, the U.S. abuses the most, despite having a higher minimum legal alcohol drinking age than many comparable developed countries. Alcohol is the third leading cause of death in the U.S.

Alcohol disordered adults abuse their kids 4 times more

It's estimated that 17 million Americans have an alcohol use disorder (AUD). This is a medical term that includes overt alcoholism, AND drinking that does not appear to have caused dependency. Less than 15% of these individuals with alcohol use disorder EVER seek treatment.

Children live with ALCOHOL IMPAIRED, and violent and abusive, adults, in unsafe homes.

What is neglect?

Some parents, caregivers, and step-parents, resent having to care for kids or young teens, and leave the house after cleaning the cupboards out of food – leaving none for the kids – and drive away to visit a friend for two days. The child or pre-teen is left with no money, and no transportation, and is very, very lucky if they have a big brother or sister living nearby they can call to come buy them food. That is one form of neglect.

In situations where an adult goes through a devastating experience – a major loss – the person can sometimes experience a type of psychosis, where they feel split off from other people. When someone is overwhelmed by their own pain, they can ignore the anguish of others. When feelings of bitterness and grief combine, sometimes a person's feelings become essentially paralyzed. In this form of neglect, the adult can become callous and entirely forget about their kids.

Another form of neglect, and/or abuse, is when an 8 year old girl asked her father: "Daddy do you love me?" his answer was: "I keep a roof over your head and I feed you, so just shut up." It is a human drive for children to want their parents to protect them. A child wants to know: do you love me? Will you find a way to keep me safe? For an adult to not pay attention and to not answer these pressing questions a child has, is a serious form of neglect.

What is abuse?

Abuse occurs when the parent or caregiver exerts their will for POWER-OVER the child, without caring emotionally for the child or the child's desires. A simpler explanation is when the adult or abuser uses the child to meet a desire or need that the adult has, using the child as a free "extension of oneself" – like a little affectionate robot that *ought* to do what the parent asks.

In situations where an adult goes through a devastating experience – a major loss – the person can sometimes experience a type of psychosis, where they feel split off from other people. When someone is overwhelmed by their own pain, they can ignore the anguish of others. When feelings of bitterness and grief combine, sometimes a person's feelings become essentially paralyzed. In this form of neglect, the adult can become callous and entirely forget about their kids.

From the child or pre-teen's point of view, being neglected or abused causes HEARTACHE. The hurt comes from the emotional betrayal of being hurt by someone the child was forced to give *undeserved trust* – to a weak, selfish, mentally ill, adult.

So one mother with a 7 month old baby, was constantly carrying it around when company was visiting, and casually bumping into the wall – with the baby's head bumping into the wall. Then the mother would say, as the baby cried, "Oh, sweetie, here let Mommy kiss it." The mother may have been doing it to draw attention to herself – she was a Mommy, and she had made a baby. Is it abuse, to use a child this way? Is she endangering the child's health or safety? Yes.

This constant bumping the baby's head could have caused concussions, but the mother did not take the child to be examined for it. It was pointed out to the father, but he and his wife were in a constant "cold war" and he didn't want to talk to her about ANYTHING, and they had stopped sleeping together. The mother would often finish off a complete bottle of wine by herself, in the evening, so she had an alcohol abuse problem, and sleeping with her was likely unpleasant.

This mother's injuring the child, if she had been taking it to the doctor, to get attention from the doctor – since she seemed to be seeking attention – would be an example of the mental disorder Munchausen's By Proxy Syndrome, where a parent – usually a mother but can be a father too – will injure a child then take it to the doctor so that the doctor will pay attention to the attention-starved parent.

This mother went on to sleep for 4 years with her youngest child, who hated it, and so she finally stopped that. Then she started sleeping at night with her daughter who was 11 and slept in her bed until she was 13. Shortly after the girl hit 13, she started occasionally sleep-walking downstairs, all the way into the living room. Sleepwalking is a sign of severe stress.

The estimated annual cost of child abuse is more than 124 BILLION dollars.

- Kids whose parents abuse alcohol and other drugs are kids who were 3 times more likely to be abused and more than 4 times more likely to be neglected than kids in non-abusing families.
- More than 2/3 of people treated for drug abuse, reported being neglected or abused as kids.
- Children who experience abuse are 9 times more likely to become involved in criminal activity.

- The F.B.I. reports that <u>every day</u> more than 100,000 kids under the age of 18, stand by U.S. freeways trying to hitch rides to run away.
- For girls, 1 out of 4 under the age of 18 expected to experience sexual abuse or assault, and 1 out of 5 boys.
- Sports Illustrated Magazine published an article where reporters found that an abusive coach – coaching both sex children in any sport – would on average, *abuse 120 kids* before the end of their career.

What triggers adults to become violent in their abuse?

Different reasons cause caretakers or parents to become violent to children. Alcohol often plays a BIG part in any sexual abuse done to children – it's a factor 80% of the time. Being hit or verbally put-down, can be caused by substance-abusing adults too, or just adults who have become totally <u>impulsive</u> –without good mental control. One out of 4 U.S. citizens is considered mentally disturbed enough to warrant medical attention – that's untreated, un-medicated, mental illness of various sorts.

Some parents, through mental illness, exhaustion, or depression, <u>run out of energy and ability to cope with children</u>. Researchers surveying 1,000 U.S. mothers with children between 2 and 10, found that young kids asked 11 questions an hour, such as: "Why is the sky blue? How do fish breathe underwater?" It averaged out to a question every 2 minutes, or 12 hours a day of questions. An exhausted adult can feel that they are just giving themselves completely away, and that they don't have anything more to give, and the parent can become enraged. Fathers would just say: "Go ask your mother."

Most children who die from abuse, are killed by parents or relatives. It can be triggered by events such as an adult shaking an infant to death because it won't stop crying, to the extent of attempted murder.

Two examples of desperately evil child abuse – deliberate attempted murder, and completed murder, follow.

People Magazine published the true account of Brryan Jackson, now 19, whose father injected Brryan with HIV-tainted blood. When he was an infant, in an attempt to evade child support.

By age 5 Brryan had full blown AIDS. Miraculously, he recovered with anti-viral drugs, grew up, is healthy, and has even forgiven his father, who has been in prison since 2006.

An example of a mother killing her children, is the Utah woman, Megan Huntsman. She had 3 daughters with her husband, who are in their late teens. Then she got pregnant 7 other times, and strangled the infants and hid them in her garage. She and her husband divorced in 2011, and it was only then that anyone looked into the boxes in the garage of dead babies.

She was – and is –mentally ill. Having 11 pregnancies under the age of 39, would indicate a person who had seriously depleted health or great ignorance about how to be healthy. Experts think she was driven to do these murders after becoming deeply depressed and unable to function like a normal person.

3 – WHAT'S BEHIND THE CRUELTY

"To err is human." William Shakespeare

The illustration at the beginning of this chapter of a criminal in prison, is a reminder that times have changed, and to abuse a child is an illegal crime, often a felony, with serious jail time, when the abusers are reported. There are reasons that with abuse rates so high, that most abusers are *not* reported to the police. Abusers often know that they are culpable – they lie and cheat and blame the victims, to shield themselves from the consequences of their crimes.

Abusers have various forms of mental illness, often showing in that they *want to feel powerful over others* and disobey rules, and who have sympathy for no one but themselves. Consider every child abuser: (1) mentally ill in some manner, (2) sociopathic in their contempt of cultural or legal rules of how to treat people, and (3) you can almost always consider <u>an abuser biologically and abnormally immature</u>!

The neglect and abuse victims – the children, are usually too scared to report their abusers. The *other adults who know about the abuse* are often *complicit* – *that means they go along with it* – sacrificing the child getting hurt rather than themselves. When children reach 18, they have a couple of years, depending upon state laws, to sue for damages from their abusers.

It is clear to anyone that if an adult is <u>abusing</u> a child or pre-teen or teen – they are not <u>loving the child</u> - no matter what they SAY to them. Some abusers typically pass the blame: "Look what you made me do", and other sexual abusers call what they do "love" and say: "…the kid came on to me, the kid was in love with me…" which (1) reveals the deep delusions that accompany these personality disorders are forms of mental illness, and (2) shows that the abuser does NOT know what love is.

Love is GIVING, not just RECEIVING. When an adult conquers a child it is the act of a weak and selfish person, often mentally ill person, as they satisfy THEIR appetite. Some of the abusers deliberately want a weak person – such as a child – so they EASILY DOMINATE THEM.

Most criminals have grown up (1) failing to BOND with anyone else in a loving way, and (2) they have daily DELUSIONS that other people don't really "mind" too much if they push them around and manipulate them or hurt them. They are abnormally immature in recognizing that there are consequences to their actions. They have a teenager's immature belief that they will get away with bad behaviors.

Different type of mental illnesses, personality disorders, and biochemical imbalances can contribute to make an adult an abuser of children. One of the types of abusers who constantly emotionally destroys children, is a narcissist who verbally does "put-downs" that (1) can destroy a child's will and trust, and (2) lead to the child committing suicide.

One newspaper reporter was married to a managing editor of the paper, who was very demanding, and a raging alcoholic when he got home at the end of the day. When he was drinking – which was every night – he would say viciously cruel things to their children. The wife wasn't ready to divorce him.

One day she drove home from work and found her fifteen year old son, hanging from a tree branch in the big tree in their front yard, dead.

As is apparent, many spouses think they are unable to intervene against a raging, violent, substance abuser, even when he – or she – is abusive.

One woman was furious at her husband who had just gotten home, and was in the kitchen to see if he could help prepare the meal. She hated cooking and wasn't good at it. Two of their 4 children were in the kitchen when she picked up a big pan of burning hot cooking oil, and threw it at him. He ducked, and wasn't burned.

They had been going for marriage counseling, but he knew that she would not agree to taking medication for her abnormal mental behaviors. She would have tantrums EVERY day, and sometimes 3 times a day.

This woman screamed at the top of her lungs at her 6- year old son and began slapping him, when he left a footprint on a newly shampooed rug, calling him: "You stupid, stupid boy! Look at the trouble you've caused!"

People who have out-of-control rage problems, are often naturally biochemically imbalanced, and they often try to "self-medicate" by drinking or taking other substances. This husband knew that she would NOT "get help", but he did fear for his life when she tried to kill him a second time, so he agreed to her request for a divorce. Which made her even MORE angry! His plan for his kids safety was to put them in boarding school, where they would be out of her control.

Many spouses get exhausted and completely burned-out, coping with spouses with mental disorders, even when they WANT to protect their kids, they feel powerless to do so. One of the types of mental disorders that is (1) quick to get angry and (2) doesn't care whom they hurt, is the person with "Narcissistic Personality Disorder."

Narcissistic Personality Disorder

(from the DSM-IV (Diagnostic and Statistical Manual of Mental Disorders)

DIAGNOSTIC FEATURES –

The essential feature of narcissistic personality disorder is a pervasive pattern of grandiosity, need for admiration, and lack of empathy that begins by early adulthood and is present in a variety of contexts."

Among the tell-tale features are:

"is uncomfortable in situations in which he or she is not the center of attention".

"displays rapidly shifting and shallow expression of emotions".

"shows self-dramatization, theatricality, and (unprovoked) emotions (like tantrums)".

"considers relationships to be more intimate than they actually are".

NARCISSIST –

"... development characterized by a love of self that PRECEDES, IF NOT PRECLUDES, LOVE OF OTHERS."

The neurosis causes the person to have an excessive need for admiration and attention, and inappropriate emotional reactions to the criticisms of others. It is a neurosis characterized by such excessive self love (following a childhood emotional injury of neglect) that NORMAL LOVE FOR OTHERS IS IMPOSSIBLE."

A MALIGNANT NARCISSIST –

A personality disorder characterized by "... suspiciousness to the point of paranoia, feelings of self-importance, and sadistic cruelty accompanied by a complete lack of remorse."

When emotional drives turn to cruelty

Human emotions fulfill different uses in different circumstances. People who escaped over the Berlin Wall or escaped from concentration camps, used their most ruthless and cunning skills – and sometimes had to kill people to escape – in order to survive. There are circumstances under which almost anyone will kill another person, including the obvious one to kill for their own survival and self preservation.

WHAT ABOUT THE VIOLENT PREDATOR? –

There are vindictive criminals in our world, who have behaved badly for many years, and who felt that they had no chance at a better life. There are isolated examples where a mentor (in one case a Massachusetts juvenile Court Judge) took a teen murderer under his guidance, and turned the kid around into an outstanding person and attorney.

Although the predator has no trust in other people – or because of having no trust – the predator may be highly charming and skilled at manipulating others. They can get helpers or followers sometimes, by weaving a web of evil around a person. But usually, the predator has been cruelly treated growing up, and trusting no one, is attached to no one compassionately, and so is criminally cruel.

The statistics on violence show a strong trend – over 50 years – of greater violence being caused by the hormone testosterone. Men have more of it than women, and commit more acts of violence. Violent women – and killer, predatory women – also have high levels of testosterone – both genders have the hormone, just in different amounts. Testosterone usually is at its highest in 17 or 18 year old males, which is why they tend to commit so many impulsive acts at that age, some resulting in harming or killing others, and because of the high testosterone, there has not been a time in history when armies have not been able to recruit young men of this age, to do the violent work of soldiers.

EMOTIONAL DRIVES –

There are many variations on the basic human emotions and human drives, but according to the in-depth research done by William Glasser, M.D., there are FOUR very deeply conditioned, and motivating drives. Some of these cause cruelty and some of these cause deep compassionate caring.

Generally, the more "playful" – and callously regarding other people as playthings – attitude combined with a HIGH drive to be competitive, and powerful, and have high personal freedom (be BEYOND society's (rules) combines to fuel the drive of greatest cruelty.

FOUR DRIVES – some cause love, some cause cruelty

Learning to spot and get away from cruel people. Alcohol and meth, and some other drugs, alter the human brain, and cause "Love and Belonging" compassion to be SUPPRESSED and IMPULSIVENESS to dominate, and then people behave with CRUELTY.

The more "playful" – and callously regarding other people as playthings – attitude combined with a HIGH drive to COMPETE, and have FREEDOM (be BEYOND society's (rules) combines to fuel the drive of greatest cruelty.

The psycho-biological drives that are part of a human being's survival destiny, get *distorted* by the incoming chemicals. Memory gets shut off, and compassion gets shut off – and survival and competition get turned on HIGH.

Think of the four basic drives, which include: a grid that has four squares with one square having POWER in it, one square have FUN AND COMPETITIVENESS in it, one square having FREEDOM in it, and he fourth square having LOVE AND BELONGING in it.

POWER	FREEDOM
FUN AND COMPETITIVENESS	LOVE AND BELONGING

Under the influence of alcohol and meth, and cocaine, and other substances, the body simplifies what processes it makes available to us physically – and MENTALLY – with the result that FUN AND COMPETITIENESS gest dialed up HIGH, and put together with a strong drive for FREEDOM – makes a person wildly impulsive. The gentler drive of LOVE AND BELONGING – is completely overlooked when under the influence. Having the other drives is "overdrive" with zero love and compassion = CRUELTY. That's how it happens. It's biological. Using substances can make people who are solely self-focused, super-selfish – and low on consideration or compassion for other people – including their own relatives or kids.

The young man who did the Newtown, CT, shootings, was mentally impaired on the Autism spectrum, and was very low in having feelings of "love and belonging" toward anyone, let alone kids at a school.

We learn to stop being victims and we learn to stop being addicted to EXCITEMENT.

We learn that we "stuffed" our feelings from our traumatic childhoods and have lost the ability to express our feelings because it hurts (DENIAL).

Abusing or neglecting children at home

The only preventative to abusiveness or cruelty drives at home, are if the caretaking adults have HIGH drives for Love and Belonging, which cause kindness.

In February 2014. Psychology Today published some interesting biological findings about how similar many species are – and how UNIQUELY different we are. It was found that some species do NOT HAVE GENTLENESS to a degree that humans would want to see. Chimpanzees surprisingly have a very high competitive drive. That is all about DOMINANCE. Yet humans and chimpanzees do share a factor of conscientiousness, while orangutans do not.

If an adult is under the influence of alcohol or other drugs, the self-centeredness, the drive for "fun" and "power" and "freedom" – all combine to make a VERY inconsiderate or MEAN person while under the influence. If this person is parenting, they are likely a cruel parent.

Abusing and bullying done "at home" or in the privacy of a parent's home or a foster home – is extremely difficult to restrict because:

- The official "guardian" of a child has temporary or permanent legal rights that the children do NOT have.
- The official "guardian" or AUTHORITY FIGURE, has the power to inflict an atmosphere onto children, of being in a Prisoner of War Camp – or like being *kidnap victims*.
- The official "guardian" may be low on compassion, high on aggression, very depressed, or an addict – all of which leads the "guardian" to seek out the easy-to-get dominance "high" of doing a put-down, or abusing a child or any household members.

ABUSING ADULTS -

Being abusive to kids, or other adults, by adults, is often impulsive and opportunistic, much of the time.

In road rage or regular driving when people cut drivers off – it's impulsive and opportunistic, as is cutting in line at the post office, or Federal Express, or coffee shops and other locations.

When adult abuse of adult children is deliberate

There are also "campaigns of abuse" that are <u>deliberate</u> – making a person into a "scapegoat" - not opportunistic – frequently among employers who are not mentally well. But the most frequent source of bullying campaigns comes from "loved ones" – former boyfriends, mates, spouses, or <u>most particularly among older family members</u> who are not mentally well and need professional help.

A parent who has been raging at his or her kids for years, often <u>resents</u> that an adult kid wants to be treated better – and gets MORE enraged! Some parents begin to physically slap or hit their adult kids, when they hadn't previously, because their <u>rage has increased</u> over time and they have fewer outlets for their rage to be released –as their social contacts decrease with age.

Adult children can find themselves on the receiving end of as much or more rage than they experienced in childhood. The adult child may still be allowing this abuse – giving UNDESERVED TRUST to this former love or relative.

Some adult children decide to severely limit contact with such familiar abusers, or simply to cut and eliminate contact, when the raging "authority figure" in their family, does NOT get professional help.

Many times the raging adult has been to M.D.s for other ills, and has been advised to take anti-depressants, or other medications, to calm down their high aggression. M.D.s can see in their behavior and by their blood pressure that they need medication – and the parent or guardian REFUSES to take the meds. They do NOT want to change, because they will lose their satisfying, familiar ways of behaving.

Impact on adults from alcoholic and dysfunctional families

People who have experienced bullying, in the privacy of a parent's home or a foster home, by a parent or official "guardian", have often grown into adulthood:

- Finding it feels most <u>familiar</u> being around authority figures who are able to inflict an atmosphere of being in a Prisoner of War Camp.
- Having behavior habits that make them respond like victims, rather than survivors, and they may internally still feel they have to respond to requests or demands, like being *kidnap victims*.
- Being unaware that they GIVE people UNDESERVED TRUST, which leads to being unsafe.

Children raised in bullying or abusive environments often grow up to respond to adult bullying experiences, in the same ways as do adult kidnap victims or POWs. They all change their behaviors so that they <u>accommodate</u> or <u>co-depend</u> the abusive guardian, in order to survive in the frightening environment.

They often take this over-accommodating behavior, which is a form of super-fast bonding being co-dependent – into most arenas of their adult lives.

This type of co-depending or fast, pressured-bonding, when it's in a kidnapping environment, is called the Stockholm Syndrome, since it was first observed among kidnapped hostages in a Stockholm, Sweden, bank.

THE FIRST SET OF RESULTS –

When a child survives to the age of 18 and legally "escapes", they have had years of conditioning in:

(1) Fear of authority figures.
(2) Having a lack of assertiveness and self-protective skills (which is sometimes referred to as a lack of "boundaries").
(3) Often believing they have to keep this abusive treatment secret – which postpones recovery.
(4) Having a deeply ingrained habit of GIVING to other people – as they did to the "guardian" – UNDESERVED TRUST.

THE FINAL RESULT –

Abuse continues to happen to these "Adult Children", when they are adults if they do not STOP giving UNDESERVED TRUST to other people.

For recovery, they must acquire assertiveness skills – the biggest one of which is learning to say "No!" to people - setting boundaries skills to defend themselves from unsafe people.

They must learn to distinguish levels of trustworthiness, in order to protect themselves like healthy adults do, and NOT do any more giving of UNDESERVED TRUST.

Substances and biology that cause brain problems

Many forms of aggression in the most psychopathic, or most mentally damaged and VIOLENT, are due to physical abnormalities or biochemical abnormalities that make an abuser, rapist, or killer have no conscience or compassion.

In the earliest research days of the field of psychology, scientists were mesmerized by a former train foreman who had been kind and respected, who was injured as a railroad spike went into his brain. When the spike was touched, such that it pushed on certain brain sectors, he became uncontrollably violent.

Some babies are born with skull malformations, or in the process of a difficult delivery, have their soft skills misshapen, and that can injure sensitive sections of the brain, and cause behavior problems. Harvard has found that the lack of good fetal nutrition, even causes lasting behavior problems. It has been found that any substance abuse, and particularly nicotine, that is ingested during gestation, can result in kids having ADD or ADHD behavior problems, as a result of the nicotine their tiny bodies cannot repel.

Police and law officers have long known about certain families that are habitual criminals NOT JUST BECAUSE OF FAMILY TRAINING, but because of malformed skills. One family of 3 generations of repeat offenders – call them the "Jones family" – each had a forehead – and the frontal lobe behind it where rational thought occurs – that was only an inch high. They didn't just look like some ape-like creatures from the past – they literally did not HAVE the mental capacities in their smaller skulls – that modern man had developed.

There are locations for anxiety and fight or flight – the amygdala – and there are hormones – testosterone – that INCREASE violence in people.

Humans have their behavior modified not only by <u>what</u> they are taught, but also by the size of the INSULA region that develops in the brain. This develops to give a person compassion, and to help them feel happiness.

It is stimulated by holding small animals and playing with them and by being held, and by lots of friendly eye contact <u>from people who are encouraging to them</u>! Any person who is deprived of these stimulants has a tiny or non-existent insula region, is unhappy, and wants others to feel as miserable as they do – and <u>they have no conscience or developed compassion</u> toward others!

THE U.S. IS UNREGULATED FOR YOUNG PEOPLE'S SAFETY -

MS. Magazine published a statistic about young girls going to college, that 1 in 5 would be molested on college campuses. College campuses have their own security forces, that they use to avoid bad publicity that would affect enrollment. They under-report the crimes that occur and they do not report them to the local municipal police.

A risk for young boys, freshman particularly, is when a coach is sexually abusive – such as the Pennsylvania coach Sandusky. Sports Illustrated reported that in an average career, each abusive coach sexually molests an average of 130 boys.

Olympic champion boxers Sugar Ray Leonard and Mike Tyson have both reported that they were sexually abused as young boys.

EXAMPLE:

Jeanette was a shy, petite, blond, who was a freshman at college, and very introverted. She had grown up close to her father and brother, while her mother had been put into an institution for her advanced Alzheimer's disease. Jeanette's life experience had been confined to home and family.

In the dorm at the college, being shy, she made a friend of a boy who was down the hall, and they talked about homework for the most part for 6 months. She had no romantic feelings for him. One afternoon, he came into her room, she was not expecting anything but their normal conversation, and he shoved her down on her single bed and raped her.

She was so traumatized and shocked she didn't even report the incident. She just immediately dropped out of that school and transferred to a day school near her home. With so little experience and having given him so much underserved trust – which is what abusers COUNT on from victims – he said that if she ever reported it he'd say she led him on and that it was consensual sex."

# # #

Clearly by all his quick verbal comebacks, this was not his first time at the rapists "rodeo", and he knew how to isolate young girls of inexperience, which would give HIM fewer problems, in his POWER-OVER domination thrill which rape provides.

All forms of POWER-OVER others, give a biochemical "high" or "rush", which people often experience playing aggressively competitive games or sports.

THERE ARE HELPFUL DRUGS TO MODERATE DESTRUCTIVE BEHAVIOR –

Alcohol and other recreational drugs are a disaster because the drugs let the nervous system override the rational mind.

There are, fortunately, different drugs that can help. Some drugs have to be taken for an entire lifetime, others not. These pharmaceutical drugs reduce the anxiety in the brain that causes cravings.

In France, an eminent physician who served the President of France, Dr. Olivier Ameisen, wrote an amazing book: "The End of My Addiction." He had developed a problem with alcohol abuse to try to calm himself down after stressful work, and temporarily destroyed his professional life. He spent several years researching options, and found that the drug Baclofen reduces cravings. It works with the receptors for GABA, which many stressed, or abused people, are <u>short of</u> – which is why they self-medicate. The drug works on many, many people. Dr. Ameisen continues to be an expert in cardiology, was affiliated with Cornell in the U.S., and practices in the U.S. and Paris.

What alcoholics and other addicts are looking for

Most addicts want the (1) feeling of numbed out forgetfulness, of their past pains and disappointments, and (2) dopamine, the endorphin hormone of FEELING PLEASURE.

This biochemical HIGH is what the rapist or abuser looks to get from dominating another person. They make another person feel smaller, *so they can feel taller*. The feeling is OVER others – or domination – and in some people, it is biochemically a MUCH STRONGER DRIVE than in other people.

Hormones go all over the place, with the result usually of the hormone testosterone – for strength and cruelty – and adrenaline – for survival – being called up in HUGE amounts.

Contrarily, many alcoholics find that when they quit drinking, they quit being violent. The facts say 80% of violence in the U.S. is committed under the influence of alcohol, and this includes child abuse.

Drugs reduce a person's mental capacities – often permanently; alcohol corrupts a person's conscience.

Since the majority of child abuse or neglect is directly connected to substance abuse, consider the ramifications of substance abuse.

In the U.S., since more than 2/3 of people treated for drug abuse, reported being neglected or abused as kids, it is clear that parents and grandparents can have endured very dysfunctional and cruel upbringings, that they follow, out of ignorance, with following generations.

Children who have been raised around substance-abusers with such inattentive or cruel child-care practices – actually child-abuse practices – are 3 times more likely to be abused and more than 4 times more likely to be neglected than kids in non-abusing families.

ADDICTS –

Street drugs are strange substances, and create a lot of people who are solely self-focused, super-selfish – low on consideration or compassion for other people, including their own relatives or kids. They can mercilessly try to extort attention and "suck out" optimism from anyone around who is feeling more high energy than them – even USING mere children.

People who use substances have their behavior <u>biologically changed</u> by the substance they take. There are psycho-biological drives that are part of a human being's survival destiny, and get *distorted* by the incoming chemicals. Memory gets shut off, and compassion gets shut off – and survival and competition get turned on HIGH.

The influence an alcoholic has on a young victim

Many kids who have been in domestic violence homes or domestic prisoners of war have been so terrified, that like soldier prisoners of war, they use up all their B vitamin stores, and don't have a shredded nerve left. They are "frozen" in terror and in <u>low energy</u>. They may not have GABA left after their GABA receptors have been so abused – to be able to sleep deeply without help.

If they sleepwalk, it indicates that there is not enough GABA in their systems, since GABA is supposed to incapacitate the lower limbs from moving <u>so that human beings can get sleep</u>.

So these neglected and abused children have endured different degrees of fear and even terror. With after-effects that incapacitate them and demand treatment.

When parents want to conceal their "bad habits" which is what one alcoholic father called his drinking and smoking, the kids are forced to "keep secrets", and if they ever made a critical remark they were told by angry parents to: "Put a cork in it!"

Children can be EXHAUSTED emotionally by the demands alcoholics make. The alcoholic is particularly attached to getting SYMPATHY. They are constantly looking for an opportunity to feel wronged so they can have a SELF PITY PARTY. The world allows for all sorts of people, and all sorts of situations. There are some people who only want to RECEIVE – not GIVE – such as those receiving sympathy. If they remain "weak" they can continue to *receive sympathy and attention*, with no reciprocity involved – they don't have to give anything *back to other people*.

Watch out for the after-effects of being raised around alcoholics

Alcoholics are renowned by alcohol experts as:

- Being <u>extremely resistant to change</u> – including NOT quitting drinking – even when life-saving health or therapy requires it.
- They are <u>selfish</u> – they want to feel "better" themselves no matter how anybody else feels. One alcoholic woman used to take a small pint bottle out of her purse, which she would keep by her chair, and take secret sips from, and drink all during her visits with her sister. She worked for the police department.
- Alcoholics don't CARE what happens to their "victims" because alcohol <u>kills compassion</u>, and they only care about THEIR OWN feelings.
- One father was called to the emergency ward of the college hospital when his son had passed out on the library steps from alcohol poisoning. At the hospital, two fraternity brothers gave the father an earful saying what a "terrible father he was, and how he ignored and let his son down in a disgraceful way". The father was already half in the bag from his normal nightly drinking, but he did repeat what was said sort of marveling that anybody would say such negative things about HIM. He <u>only thought of himself</u>. And he was conscious that his self image in the eyes of others had been disrespected. Image counts a LOT to many alcoholics, since

alcohol causes EMOTIONAL SELF INFLATION –
delusions of superiority over other people.

- Many alcoholics, with their <u>extreme self-centeredness</u>, are akin to "Domestic Terrorists" – being so inconsiderate as to frequently and casually be hurting others to get attention for their own hurts,
- They can seem "fun-loving" to some other drinker pals, but mostly the playfulness is actually that they are <u>immature</u>. They were typically neglected or abused as children and so began drinking at such early ages (13-14) – that they LACK and <u>missed out on adult skills</u>. They don't have the skills for themselves, <u>and did not pass them on or show them</u> to their offspring,
- Alcoholics have a favorite type of party – usually accompanied by drinking – but it is their FAVORITE type of party. They <u>love self-pity parties</u>. They <u>want other people</u> to provide them *consolation and affectionate attention* – for how bad they feel when they self pity. When they feel bad, it is RARELY out of conscience <u>for how they make other people feel bad</u>, it is disappointment – self-pity for <u>how bad THEY feel</u>.
- Alcohol destroys some brain sector functioning, and removes some of the endorphins they need to <u>reduce pain.</u> So alcoholics – particularly when they are hung-over for several hours the next day after drinking – literally HURT more than normal people. Their "normal" pain killers have been maimed and killed off by the excessive amounts of hormones rushing in every time they drink, and so the pain killing receptors don't work anymore. They have to take pharmaceutical drugs, such as anti-depressants, or they have to take supplements such as the B vitamin pantothenic acid, (used by alcoholism treatment experts) to <u>reduce the pain they feel</u>.

- Alcohol impairs memory, in some cases, permanently. Sectors of the brain for memory – just the like the pain reducing facilities – DO NOT COME BACK EVER.

THIS IS ALL VERY IMPORTANT TO THE SURVIVORS!

4 – IT'S NOT YOUR FAULT - BE A SURVIVOR

"Nothing can dim the light that shines from within."

Maya Angelou

There are chapters in this book about skills, how to accelerate personal change, how to grieve and mourn your losses, find your strengths, deal with cruelty when you encounter it, and when and how much to trust people. The poet quoted at the open of this chapter lived a life of many hardships, including sexual abuse while still a young woman. She survived her pain, and was an example to millions of people that once you find your inspiration, your life can unfold in miraculous ways once you speak your truth.

In terms of recognizing what is true, you can know when to trust, at those moments when what you're thinking in your head matches what you're feeling in your heart, you are probably getting a consistent message to either trust, or not trust – that you can rely on. Listen to your heart.

> *"You will never be able to escape from your heart. So it's better to listen to what it has to say."*
>
> *Paolo Coelho*

This book has a little bit of everything that is needed to learn, to heal faster.

REMEMBER THAT almost 80% of U.S. families do neglect, emotional, sexual, or physical abuse to the children who live in those households. IT IS NOT YOUR FAULT !

It is important for victims, and survivors of child neglect and abuse, involving substance abuse and violence, to understand how mentally ill their caretakers were. This does NOT excuse the caretakers.

80% of neglected and abused kids have Post Traumatic Stress Disorder, that needs treatment. Looking for symptoms of Post Traumatic Stress Disorder is one of the clearest ways to identify that neglect or abuse occurred, even when the child blocked it out and has no memory of it happening.

PTSD Symptoms range from breathing difficulties, hernias, sleep problems to complete insomnia, to ringing in the ears, to forms of behavior that may seem like Aspergers or autism, or conduct disorder, or being schizoid and uncommunicative – and they all flinch at loud noises.

Children who have been raised around substance-abusers with such inattentive or cruel child-care practices – actually child-abuse practices – are 3 times more likely to be abused and more than 4 times more likely to be neglected than kids in non-abusing families.

If you were exposed to caretakers or relatives who used alcohol, drugs, or other substances to excess, you may have experienced some forms of cruelty, first-hand, that are difficult to imagine. One father shot at his teenage sons in the driveway, putting a slug in each of their calves. And the neighbors didn't call the cops.

And if he was drunk enough, he genuinely would not remember doing it the next day.

KEEP IN MIND: IT'S NOT YOUR FAULT

Identify the trauma reaction style

One of the best books on trauma, titled "Trauma" by Judith Herman, Ph.D., covers the *damage done to people* in war, domestic traumas, and rape traumas, and outlines recovery strategies – that are similar for all types.

There are commonly three victim reaction styles to trauma:

- One type isolates and hides, almost becoming autistic in their unwillingness to communicate. This is sometimes called a "somatic" style since other atypical behaviors or illnesses, such as being schizoid or being Aspergers-like, can result. This type can hide inside themselves and learn a lot of information, and so can find their way in life based on the information and intelligence they develop. Their social skills are usually abnormally under-developed – bordering on the pre-adolescent. They "hide" to not be re-victimized.

- Another type of trauma victim tries to push around other people – sometimes with even charm and humor – but constantly seeks to be in control not just of his or herself, but to have control over others. This victim victimizes other people throughout their lives. It can be bullying, abuse, or being predatory.
- A third type of victim is one who has survived by becoming "co-dependent" with most people they interact with – doing for others – looking for praise and acceptance – and *protection* – from the other person in exchange. They are often disappointed and they are often re-victimized again and again. They are sometimes called "the pleaser".

EXAMPLE:

A television reality program teenage mother described her experiences that could be categorized as having been an undefended "pleaser", who has been re-victimized.

Her traumatic past includes being raped twice, including by a new boyfriend, that resulted in having an abortion on her 16th birthday, getting pregnant again.

She is now writing a book about her experiences to show her children that no matter what you go through, you can come out of it alright.

# # #

Recovery options to be informed about

Dr. Judith Herman found that everyone recovered better after they had:

- Been in a controlled small, same sex confidential group of similarly damaged survivors.
- She also found that the first step to recover is to be "witnessed" by others that there was injury.
- Some people can find group counseling sessions, or even find a 12-step group that can provide the WITNESSING step for them. EACH PERSON MUST FIND THEIR OWN PATH through either a bridge made of planks of new skills, walking around the big mountains of pain blocking them, or hopping onto different 12-steps – there are as many different ways to be on your journey back to strength, as there are people.
- Some people benefit from going to martial arts/rape clinic crisis arrangements where a man dresses up in a padded suit and each woman gets to hit the guy with a stick as long and as hard as she wants.
- Some people benefit from a daily "anger and frustration" session, where they take a plastic bat and hit their mattress or a pillow to get out their feelings for the day – and they use their lung muscles in hitting the pillow, and the lung muscles are a storage spot for a lot of old pain – which otherwise causes shallow breathing and other ills.
- After a traumatic event, particularly after being maimed or violated, or raped, it can take 2,300 hours of crying to GRIEVE the psychic pain out of the body. Watch a sad movie such as "Running with Scissors", or "People Like Us", "Terms of Endearment", or "The Hereafter", "My Life as A Dog", "Prince of Tides".
- Canada used B12 shots, given frequently for the rest of their lives, to recovered prisoners of war who were severely traumatized. Getting B12 shots reduces the symptoms of

PTSD and increases the lung's breathing which expels stored fear and pain.

- Massage can be profoundly releasing. Gentle massage is one of the first techniques used to help tortured prisoners of war recover, when they get treatment in Denmark, the center for the world's torture victims.
- Dr. Herman found that eventually people could start re-entering regular life, and begin trusting people, after they began simple WORK. The research found that ALL victims move on to becoming survivors when they feel some <u>value for having contributed</u> some work. It can be tiny, tiny efforts, such as sorting nuts into different bowls – but by *doing something that was considered "useful"*, the victims began to see their own *value* again, as human beings. Volunteer work can provide this if paid work is not a possibility.
- Working – volunteering at a rape crisis clinic, or domestic violence center, or being on a crisis hotline – they give you training – helps people feel they have contributed and are less helpless. Become an ADVOCATE in the area in which you were victimized.
- The wound of humiliation and violation of abuse is repaired by doing simple work –because the humiliation wound can only be healed by seeing a person's efforts valued by others, so one can value oneself.
- Be wary of mere sympathy which is sort of like blowing cool air on a burn on the skin. There is temporary relief. The reality for the burn to heal is to have the remaining toxic elements cleaned out, and the wound be <u>protected</u>. Sympathy <u>does not</u> heal. It takes removing the internal elements that irritate the wound, and a skilled professional to "dress" the wound and teach the patient how to keep it <u>protected</u>.
- Exercise can help enormously. One woman combined her half hour walk-runs with crying – and even CRYING makes endorphins – as does moving – so she felt much BETTER.

Whenever a person walks, let alone runs, these hormones have been found in Israeli research to be as effective at countering depression, as pharmaceutical anti-depressants.

- Build in some laughter and inspiration. Watch movies such as "Airplane", "Our Idiot Brother", "Blades of Glory", "Last Chance Harvey", "The Help", "Saving Mr. Banks", "Martian Child", "The Royal Tannenbaums", "The Other Woman", "Dumb and Dumber."

Take action to heal yourself – leave other people's problems alone

The hardest thing, is to accept the limitations of what we can do. What you <u>can</u> do, is to <u>defend yourself</u> against the damages of the mentally ill. You may have to move away from them. Statistics say in the U.S., 1 out of 4 people needs mental health treatment due to mental illness. Another statistic is that an additional 25% of the population is sociopathic – that is a rule-breaker personality – hardly oriented to being good caretakers.

Adults who have not been raised in functional homes themselves, are often "neglectful", but it can be difficult to understand what was neglectful. In a recent May 5th 2014 publication, an excerpt from a recent "reality show" custody dispute released court claims of child neglect: "…Respondent, especially, in recent times, has been very neglectful in her care for the children. This has resulted in the children not getting prompt medical care, nutritional meals, hygienic care, and deterioration in their school work and attendance." In social media, the 15 year-old daughter said to her mother: "you treat me like sh*t". The mother countered, "What have I done that you hate your own mother? I gave you life and went through a horrible life change (divorce) and all you care about is yourself?"

This shows the psychological aspects of abuse to the child:

- Expecting a child, with no ability to escape financially or legally, to be content with being ignored.
- It shows that the mother thinks that giving biological birth gives her big brownie points that the child and others should admire her for! That's a mentally ill narcissistic personality disorder.
- The mother actually EXPECTS SYMPATHY from a child for the mother's OWN CHOICES – divorce, even though they caused her discomfort. Highly inappropriate and immature for an adult.

Family members may remain untrustworthy

Recovering from abuse and neglect also requires that one discover what is healthy and "courteous" and "reciprocal" and "trustworthy" human treatment between people – since abusive environments do not regularly show those traits.

It can be difficult to accept, but some parents are doing "scams" – that are illegal. One father just put stolen license plates on his 16-year old's new KIA car. The plates, according to the police, belong to a stolen truck in the northern part of the state. Another father is doing an IRS scam, where he is deducting all 3 boys who have not lived at home with him for 5 years. Another woman is taking lots of state child support money, although her ex-husband gave her $50,000 that year. Her mother-in-law felt like turning her in – but didn't do it. Another woman has her 91-year old mother living in her house – and has legal power of attorney over her mother's money. This daughter has bought herself a $26,000 facelift, and some expensive vacations. This is financial fraud – a form of elder abuse that is illegal and has fines and jail time attached.

It can be very difficult for kids or adults of dysfunctional homes, to really "see" and admit to themselves, that their relatives are basically criminals who have not been caught.

One example in this book is of a man with 2 Ph.D.s who has a responsible research scientist job, who has a brother in jail. Everyone grows at a different rate, because each of us, has a different journey in our life. For many of us, however, some good advice from professional advisor Tony Leggett is: "Stay out of your sibling's life."

Facets of forgiving - forgive to move forward

Forgiveness is a complex, and entirely personal decision for each individual to make. Clarify forgiveness by these three facets:

FACET ONE –

The person who has hurt you, or continues to hurt you, is not looking for you to forgive them if they have not expressed remorse. In a one-sided relationship, you don't benefit. It could be wise to step back emotionally and become disengaged from someone's insults or rage. To stay engaged only allows you to be hurt more and the abuser may not ever express remorse.

FACET TWO -

If you disconnect from a person who harms you – if you reduce your "emotional investment" – you are reclaiming your energy for your own recovery and increased happiness. The fastest way to do this is to do a "general forgiveness" or sort of a "general pardon", where you are not looking for any revenge or apologies. The attitude is to forgive to move forward, and to keep an emotional attitude of "Live and let live."

FACET THREE –

To make these positive changes "stick", so you continue to move forward in your recovery from past pain, it is helpful to: (1) examine the extent of your grief and to express it to relieve it; (2) understand that anger is a signal to you to protect yourself and can be motivating; and (3) avoid being sucked down the drain of hatred – it can consume so much energy it can destroy a person.

Assess your damage, then re-educate yourself to be a survivor

There can be enormous resistance to admitting that we bear scars – or are incapacitated in any way – or that we even "look" like we've been abused, but putting your head in the sand like an ostrich can leave you exposed to be bitten on the backside! There are, however, very REAL "tell-tales'" of abuse, that a trained counselor can see at first meeting you. It's best that you find out for yourself, as soon as you can.

EXAMPLE:

One handsome in his early 30s man, was walking with his sister, and a "street person" came up to them and started talking at them, the sister asked the guy to leave them alone. The guy went ballistic and started shouting: 'You think you're so much better than me! But you're not! You're assholes."

The brother was rather shaken. And then they heard a car engine start up, and the guy drove off in a dark red car – having gotten his LET'S MAKE SOMEONE FEEL SMALLER SO I CAN FEEL TALLER for the day "fix" – off of a stranger.

He wasn't even a street person. The brother asked: "Is there something printed on my forehead or something?" The sister said that yes, in fact, abused kids do show signs in their body language.

# # #

This man had been the family "scapegoat", was verbally put-down thousands of times, and physically beaten about once a week. He had a permanent ring of white showing around his iris – like a frightened horse about to run way – because he was ALWAYS being hyper-vigilant.

He, naturally, had Post Traumatic Stress Disorder, as 80% of neglected and abused U.S. kids do – which they take into adulthood.

The traits show PHYSICALLY. Go down the following checklist.

Physical, psychological, or sexual clues to abuse

Counselors and therapists and recovery group folks, have long been aware that many of the symptoms of Post Traumatic Stress Disorder are "tell-tales" that give away that a person has survived abusive trauma. Here are a few physical clues:

- Nervous eye ticks.
- Child hernias – where a kid grips their gut so hard being braced for the next hit, that they make a hernia.
- A white ring around the eye. Caused by being hit, or threatened to be hit, so often they lived in fear of it for years.
- Sleep disorders, from night terrors to sleepwalking to insomnia.
- Being overweight on purpose to make oneself unattractive to the sexual abuser in their life.
- Being "jumpy", nervous or hyper-vigilant.
- Having super-acute hearing – it's a protective measure.
- Talking too much and standing too close to people to "hold the floor". Comes from trying to entertain them or dominate them to prevent them from dominating you.
- Interrupting people when they are speaking in order to KEEP control.
- Stuttering when speaking.
- Speaking in a monotone, or trying to not talk at all.
- Not looking people directly in the eye.
- Lowering the head as if trying to avoid a slap.
- Standing with shoulders slightly curved, as if to protect the chest from being hit.
- A habit of crossing arms over chest in a protective gesture – it's defensive and can look angry.
- Using the threat of blowing up in angry tantrums, to control people to do things your way.

- Flinching at being touched by someone and surprised.
- Dislike of being touched by strangers, may not shake hands, a disease called "sensory defensiveness".
- Biting nails and chewing cuticles and "cutting" oneself.

A celebrity example is the actress Angelina Jolie, whose former babysitter told a journalist in a national magazine that her mother initially didn't hold baby Angelina, and ignored her and just stayed in bed all day, she was so depressed that her husband Jon Voight was having an affair with another woman and was leaving them. She had the nanny keep baby Angelina in a different apartment, she so disliked that Angelina looked just like Jon Voight. A few years later into her teens, besides taking heroin, Angelina Jolie was "cutting" herself heavily. She was a neglected child.

Assessing the damage to you done by alcoholics or substance users

Consider the traits and effects that typically occur when a caretaker has an alcohol use disorder, and refer back to the section in the previous chapter, to clarify WHICH particular DEVELOPMENTAL SHORTAGES due to neglect and abuse, are needed to be focused on for RECOVERY.

If you are unclear about what alcoholic physical abuse is, here's an example.

EXAMPLE: Burning a child

At a dinner table, a father was on his third martini, and sitting next to his daughter with his wife sitting at the opposite end of the table. When the sister and another sister started passing their fingers through the candle flame as fast as they could for a little game, the drunken father reached out and grabbed the oldest girl's hand and held her finger in the candle flame until it blackened.

The mother at the other end of the table looked sickened.

When the daughter grew up, she asked him about it once, and he said he had zero memory of it. Alcohol really (1) does destroy memory and (2) is a very CONVENIENT SOCIAL excuse for bad behavior.
# # #

The list in the prior chapter reminds you that alcoholics become memory-impaired and how THEY CANNOT REMEMBER what they've done. They can't remember some of the good times you can remember, and they cannot remember most of the bad things they have done to inflict pain. You can recount them until you're blue in the face, and they won't remember. If you take a photo of them while they're drunk, like actor David Hasselhoff's daughter took of him and posted on the internet – then the alcoholic can SEE what they did – WHICH THEY DON'T REMEMBER DOING!

So of course, they will not APOLOGIZE to you, or feel REMORSE for their actions – because they don't believe they did anything really.

The alcoholics feeling constant self-pity for themselves, means that kids who were victimized by them were made to feel that it was their fault and were forced to feel sympathy for the abusive alcoholic. THIS IS A GIANT RED WARNING FLAG! Children of alcoholics waste huge chunks of time – sometimes many years – trying to rescue an alcoholic – friend or lover – because it is so FAMILIAR to do so – since they were forced by conditioning by their alcoholic abuser, to show PITY for the abuser's pain. They are adults – no matter how immature – and it is THEIR responsibility to grow up. And it is NOT your responsibility to help them grow up. There are professionals who are paid by tax dollars to treat people with their illnesses. Call 911 and have the cops take the abusers to the local hospital, to get it sorted out. Is it embarrassing? It shouldn't be for YOU. It's THEIR bad behavior.

YOUR RESPONSIBILITY AS A SURVIVOR IS TO HEAL ONLY YOUR PAIN –

You may also keep selecting mates or friends who are more "needy" than you and who give less to the relationship than you do, because you are used to being on a starvation diet, emotionally. It can be "unfamiliar" for a neglected or abused child to be treated fairly, or with adult "reciprocity".

This trait of "rescuing" weaker addicts, definitely needs to be taken apart by a trained professional counselor! This is deep, and complex, and long ingrained – you deserve the best mental health professionals to teach you the adult skills you need.

The alcoholic parent did not set an adult example of trust, responsibility, keeping their word and being honest, being assertive in conflict but not cruel or aggressive.

So the victim of such a neglectful and abusive household LACKS THESE SKILLS! Your life will be "frozen", or lonely, or depressed, or "stunted", until you go get a professional to teach you!

Under the influence of alcohol, meth, cocaine, and other substances, the body simplifies what processes it makes available to us physically – and MENTALLY – with the result that FUN AND COMPETITIVENESS gets dialed up HIGH, and put together with a strong drive for FREEDOM – makes a person wildly impulsive. The gentler drive of LOVE AND BELONGING – is completely overlooked when under the influence. Having the other drives is "overdrive" with zero love and compassion = CRUELTY. That's how it happens. It's biological. Get out of the way of it.

Have you seen these behaviors in a household you have lived in:

1. Alcohol causes depression, and so kids may be around users who are depressed people. As a drug, it is categorized medically as a depressant.
2. Being chemically depressed, the alcohol using abuser feels BAD and wants to take it out on someone. Even when a person is depressed, they HAVE NO RIGHT to abuse anyone else.
3. Alcohol causes psycho-biochemical feelings of SELF inflation – where the person becomes very egotistical. They feel they are ENTITLED to have whatever they WANT – and this DELUSION makes them treat other people as DOORMATS.
4. Most alcoholics have themselves been abused and TRAUMATIZED. If not at home, then in the military service.
5. When under the influence of the drug, the delusions caused by alcohol often cause the drinker to PROJECT their feelings onto other people around them. So they IMAGINE being insulted or disrespected, and then get ANGRY and act out and hurt people.
6. Alcoholics - like most depressives – feed off the optimism of others – and will drain a person dry OF ENERGY, if they can.

Invest in taking care of yourself

Seriously pay attention to your feelings. Corrosive feelings of anxiety and anger definitely need to be controlled in order to heal. Such feelings are stimulated in the amygdala of the brain – one of the older parts of the brain that is attuned to fight or flight. Anxiety can be corrosive to your health, so you need to find a way to dial down what makes you anxious or unhappy.

One way to get through painful feelings quickly, is to JOURNAL each day. The format is that you HAND WRITE 20 times – you do NOT type – on a piece of paper:

> *"Even though I'm upset and distressed by the situation, things don't stay the same for long, the "bad guys" usually slip up and get found out, and I have lots of adult strengths that I can apply, and I have a RIGHT to be treated well and to be here."*

Make up your own script, but you get the point. A research study found that people who journaled this way found better jobs 4 months faster than their peers. These were people who wanted to overcome working with bad bosses or relationships, also, and were able to make healthy changes very quickly.

If you find yourself not able to come up with good enough reasons to protect yourself from people that do NOT have your best interests at heart, it's time to go to the best counselor or therapist you can find.

Scientific American compared research results and found that therapists who interact highly with the patients, such as in psychodynamic therapy (there is even a "short-term" form of psychodynamic therapy), – got results for patients much more quickly than cognitive therapy, where the therapist is less actively involved with the patient.

EMDR has been used successfully on Post Traumatic Stress Victims, in less than a few weeks. By teaching a person to follow another person's moving finger, or by teaching a person to tap their knees alternately – you are *interrupting a mental habit* of emotionally welling up to a painful thought, or memory. You are *changing the focus to another sensation*, and lessening the impact of the anxious thought or memory – which is how the trauma is reduced.

Using the EFT – Emotional Freedom Technique (free on the Internet), one learns to tap the eyebrows and cheekbones and hands, in ways that ALSO distract from the anxious thought At the same time, you say to yourself affirming statements such as "I'm an adult now, I have skills to handle this." Also, walking up a steep hill, pulls blood to the lower body, and a person calms down.

Look out for your own health after being depleted by being around such under-functioning people. Take lots of the mineral zinc (30-60 milligrams per day) and lots of B vitamins, so you can MAKE enough feel-good "dopamine" in your own body, to FEEL GOOD without substances. If you feel foggy-brained – low on the neuro-hormone serotonin which regulates good decision-making – eat an egg! Or take a short nap, you'll wake up with higher levels of serotonin. Or do some yoga, or meditating – these also MAKE more serotonin.

If you're looking for the "dopamine" endorphin hormone of FEELING PLEASURE, you can also kiss someone, pet a soft furry animal, sing, dance, or do jumping jacks!

TAKE <u>CARE</u> OF <u>YOU</u>! And remember: SERIOUSLY, IT'S NOT YOUR FAULT!

> *"There is nothing noble about being superior to some other person. True nobility lies in being superior to your former self."*
>
> *Indian proverb*

5 – TRUE STORIES OF CHILD ABUSE

"Suffer little children, and forbid them not, to come unto me…"

Mathew 19:14

Many generations of people have survived dysfunctional relationships and done injuries to their families, without having any idea that those behaviors are "bad" or indicative of defective hearts and poor mental health.

Some people have had a greater burden growing up being somebody's kid, than other children who had more mild experiences.

Sometimes there is a morass of agony that it is difficult to imagine anyone surviving. The wonder is that the majority of abused kids grow up to bend over backwards to not inflict pain on other people, and many become professional counselors and mental health healers.

Some kids who are sexually abused – about 15% work as adults in the sex trade – have not "gotten over" being sexually abused. Some kids who were beaten and made to feel worth nothing, descended into the hell of criminal behavior and inflicting pain on others – but they are the minority.

Some parents, particularly in the neglect category, grew up to be abnormally immature, and focused on their own pleasure and comforts, with no thought to what children need. And children need a LOT of PROTECTING – and many adults who have children, have not learned how to do that.

Many of the kids true stories that follow, have had positive adult lives. Happily, there are many of these kids who turned the chaos of their childhood lives, into planned, secure, and safe adulthood lives. Some of those kids, who may not have gotten even telephone hotline help – still have some actions they can take, to reduce the trauma of the past, to not feel defective.

A way to know trauma occurred – look for traces of PTSD

Looking for symptoms of Post Traumatic Stress Disorder is one of the clearest ways to identify that neglect and or abuse occurred, even when the child blocked it out and has no memory of it happening. The young people who experience various forms of neglect and child abuse, emerge, 80% of the time, with some of the symptoms of Post Traumatic Stress Disorder.

PTSD symptoms range from breathing difficulties, hernias, and sleep difficulties to complete insomnia, to ringing in the ears, to forms of behavior that may seem like Aspergers or autism, or conduct disorder, or being schizoid and uncommunicative, and flinching at loud noises.

Some of the experiences the kids found TRAUMATIC would sometimes NOT have been traumatic to an adult, so it can be difficult for an adult looking back at their childhood to know whether or not if it was abuse. One woman patient sitting down with her transactional psychologist for the first session, told him she wasn't sure what she wanted changed, but she didn't think she had been abused. In her mind, only sexual abuse was true abuse. To her great surprise, the psychologist said: "Oh, you've been abused, there's not a doubt. You grew up in an abusive household. We can fix a lot of things." She had many physical tip-offs of PTSD.

These children lived through tragedies at ages too young to have the skills to INTEGRATE, MOURN, AND REBUILD their lives, after the injuries and neglect occurred. Children lack adult skills, and need help to recover. People who go through tragedies, can remain carrying TRAUMA effects in their minds and bodies, until skilled people listen to them and help them.

It is clear that if an adult is abusing a child or pre-teen or teen – they are not loving the kid. Most of the examples are from households that had NO IDEA that therapists say: "If there is NO TRUST, there is NO FAMILY." Most abusers don't know that trust goes with love.

Repeated sexual abusers of children, often call what they do "love" and say: "…the kid came on to me, the kid was in love with me…" which reveals (1) the deep delusions that accompany these personality disorder forms of mental illness, and (2) shows that the abuser does NOT know what love is.

The following are examples of sexual abuse. In the United Sates, we owe a considerable debt to the psychologist and former priest John Bradshaw, who as a young man, ran away from a boy scout overnight trip, when the activities became sexually "abusive" in nature: some sexual molestation on the camping trip. That John Bradshaw, as a young boy knew that to be manipulated or physically touched in a sexual way was wrong – is an example of having a strong moral compass.

The traumatic event may have contributed to motivating him to help reach so many millions of people, in explaining how these childhood experiences result through <u>false blame from the abuser</u>, in putting shame upon the kid, and how that shame can hold people back in life.

EXAMPLE:

Ellen Degeneres abused by her stepfather.

Talk show host and comedian Ellen DeGeneres has spoken about being abused by her stepfather, as an adolescent. This was during the time her mother was getting treated for cancer, and Ellen didn't tell on him, because he was the financial support of their family, and it might emotionally devastate her mother who was in a fragile condition.

Years later, it is no surprise that DeGeneres has an obsessive need to buy and "flip" California mansions, since it makes her millions of dollars very quickly, and gives her POWER-OVER multiple homes – when she had NO power at home growing up. After the insecurity she lived through, being financially beholden to an abuser, she likely doesn't want to ever be financially beholden again.

# # #

EXAMPLE:

Kay stormed in the TV station where she worked as a receptionist, with steam practically rolling out of her ears, she was so angry. She just announced to everyone on the staff within hearing distance, the travesty that she had experienced in her family. She had just found out the night before, that her younger brother Johnny had been one of a bunch of little boys at their local church, who had been fondled "uncomfortably" by the priest.

NONE of the other boys told their mother, but Johnny and Kay happened to be in one of those incredibly rare "healthy" families, where people are honest, and look out for each other in protective ways.

Kay's mother had the moral courage to take the matter up through the ranks at the church, and she did not let Johnny go back to that church for any more activities.

As Kay said: "I am disgusted when I think about it. I am also frightened that only ONE boy – my little brother – felt able to tell his mother what happened, no matter what the priest had said to the other boys."

# # #

EXAMPLE:

A parent deliberately diminishing their child – Michael Jordan.

Michael Jordan has said that some of his motivation to become the best basketball player that he could possibly be – and he is one of the greatest players ever – was from being insulted as a child. Michael's father

James belittled his son's talent and did not ever give him approval, encouragement, or praise.

# # #

EXAMPLE:

A parent deliberately doing a put-down of a child.

A mother had her 12-year old daughter help her pull up weeds in their highly naturalistic garden, among the trees in their yard. The daughter pulled up something she thought was a weed – which was <u>not</u> a weed – and her mother screamed at her. "Can't you do anything <u>right</u>?" The daughter felt totally demeaned and had a hard time holding back her tears. The insult was so "total" – it covered "everything" – that is was purely cruel. Some forms of teasing and sarcasm are passed off as "humor", but this was a pure insult. It was a total put-down, and indictment of everything she did, and as a person. It was a comment that could only be intended to humiliate the daughter.

The daughter felt powerless – she didn't know what was a wildflower or a weed – she'd had no instruction. She was psychologically devastated. She got straight A's. She came straight home after school to help on anything her mother needed. She babysit younger siblings all the time, and was a girl scout. She was doing her best all the time. She believed the cruel remark – being so all-inclusive - it was proof that (a) she was not an "okay" person, and (b) that her family didn't love her. She became very focused on making friends with strangers, believing that they would not find fault with her the way anyone who "knew" her – like her parents – did.

# # #

EXAMPLE:

Comedian Jonathan Winters was emotionally abused.

Winters was a very famous genius comedian, who created all sorts of funny characters spontaneously, and gave millions of people the joy of laughter for decades. He had an alcoholic father who failed at his financial career, and then his mother divorced and got herself a job in broadcasting, which made her think she was the wittiest person in the world. She constantly put him down verbally, in front of other people, in public. Jonathan Winters said: "They were both insanely jealous of me...".

# # #

EXAMPLE:

Reality TV actress's domestic violence harmed her kids.

One of the many reality TV programs, the Real Housewives of Orange County, features a woman, that news accounts said had to divorce her husband because the domestic violence destroyed their marriage, and terrified their two young children.

It is a form of child abuse, to be exposed to domestic violence.

The former wife, Vicki Gunvalson said the then husband ran afoul of the law, and "he was an alcoholic. He abused me verbally...." And what was damaging to the children was that the years together were "filled with screaming. It was a very hard life."

This type of home life is <u>abuse</u> to the children who live in it.

# # #

EXAMPLE:

A father who concealed his abusiveness.

A news report recounted how Florida executive Darrin Campbell appeared outwardly to be an attentive dad, but he so over-controlled his son's sports activities that the kid told friends he hated baseball, and that he and his dad fought a lot and didn't get along.

Darrin apparently had a mental or emotional breakdown in recent years, and no one did anything about it.

Finally Darrin shot his wife and two young teen kids, set his house on fire, and shot himself.

# # #

EXAMPLE:

Susannah, as an adult, was a beautiful, tall redhead, who had amazing poise. She had grown up in a Boston enclave of the super-rich. Her mother's family had owned a bank for several generations. Her mother adopted her when she was a cute little infant, for the beautiful color of her red-gold hair. Her mother was a major figure in Boston society, and was on the board of the symphony and attended every prestigious musical event.

Imagine how thrilled the adoptive mother was to discover, when Susannah was only 6, that she had perfect pitch. Susannah could have her back to the piano, and when someone struck a note – she could identify it perfectly. She was immediately given the best, custom musical education a child could have. At the first opportunity that Susannah was old enough that she could audition for acceptance in the local musical conservatory, she auditioned. She did not get accepted.

Her mother was immediately uninterested in her. She stopped doing things with her, and left her to hang out with her two teenage older brothers. With that mother, it was perfection, or nothing.

By the time she reached puberty, Susannah had been put on the pool table in the guys' play room, and was raped by both her adoptive brothers and her adoptive father.

The family paid for an excellent college education for her, and gave her some expensive family jewels, but basically gave her nothing emotionally, and never apologized or initiated counseling. Susannah spent many years as an adult "wandering through the wilderness" trying to date "father figures", in a futile effort to rewrite the abuse of the past.

Her adoptive mother who owned the bank, eventually divorced that husband, and he went to live in Spain, where no one stateside cared what he did.

# # #

EXAMPLE:

Sean had been very successful in the appliance industry and had a regionally prize-winning business, and built a huge custom home overlooking the water for his family, and had been able to afford a summer home. He had also served bravely in the U.S. Navy, and was a likeable guy. At one point in time, his wife was pregnant with his 4th child, and she was not interested in any more of Sean's sexual attentions.

Sean turned his sexual attentions on his oldest child, a beautiful daughter, Barbara, and made her his captive lover for 3 years.

By the time Barbara was a freshman in college, Sean, was moving his sexual attentions to his second daughter Marilyn, and Marilyn told her mother, and everything came out. The entire family went for extensive counseling for all the boys, girls, and the parents.

That would be enough of an example of sexual abuse, but what came out many years later, was that when Sean had been a very cute looking young altar boy, a priest had molested him – and the other altar boys – and swore them all to secrecy. In the press in 2013, a Vatican source reported that 60% of the Catholic priests were homosexual.

For Sean, keeping his sexual abuse secret for decades, only poisoned his life more deeply, and made him into a sexual abuser of his own children. If it was alright for a PRIEST to do, then wasn't it alright?

# # #

EXAMPLE: A YOUNG GIRL SEXUALLY ABUSED

When she was just a little girl, Shawna, was constantly hit and yelled at by her beautiful mother, during the day when her father wasn't home. As soon as Shawna was old enough for kindergarten, her mother went back to work, where she adored being admired for her brunette beauty. She was specifically hired as a focal point, because she was the most beautiful woman in the store, and made customers impressed by the furniture that was sold.

Her father defended his little daughter every weekend, and every evening after he got home from work, from his angry wife's beating up on his beautiful little blond girl. The mother saw the daughter as a RIVAL, and was demeaning, cruel, and non-protective. She also punished her husband for his affection for his daughter by freezing him out.

The father eventually sexually abused his daughter. This was a family of TWO Borderline personality disorder parents, BOTH adults were competing for the love and admiration they wanted – and PUNISHING when they didn't get it. As a young teen, Shawna started locking her bedroom door to keep her father from continuing to come into her bedroom and sexually molest her.

# # #

EXAMPLE: A FATHER OR A BIG BROTHER

"There were times in my life when I really could have used a father's help, and I told myself that he didn't help, because he traveled a lot for business. But then I started really looking hard at how things shook out.

He constantly wanted attention, and he didn't give the same amount back – parent to child. He started patting me on the butt when I was quite young, graduating to real ass-grabbing butt-slapping as hard as he could – when no one was watching – in my pre-teens. He also started doing really super-mean verbal put-downs, from the age that I was enjoying school, on, for the rest of his life. So from age 9 on, every night at the dinner table he would say: 'you don't know what you're talking about.'

There was no EXCHANGE with him. It was what HE wanted.

He also told me things to make himself feel better – a forced confidant – when I was only twelve. He told me about how he had this hemorrhoid operation – really gross. And he told about pulling constipated shit out of his girlfriend's bottom – when I was still a kid. And the most horrible, was when I was a teen, he told me in excruciating detail about when my mother died in the hospital and her heart kept beating. He was just doing this cruel, HEART-WRENCHING description to a young, daughter about her mother dying, so he could UNLOAD HIS junk. Zero consideration, and zero protection of his child. He flunked as a father."

# # #

EXAMPLE:

"When my youngest brother left for college out-of-state, I was not surprised a couple of years later when he told me that he had stolen some of the gold coins in my father's collection. He obviously felt he was "owed" for the lack of fatherly support, and for being subject to a psychopath-type stepmother, while my father flew away on business trips.

I got tired of my father calling me on weekends, after I'd had a hard week working in my sales job, and he would just want to UNLOAD. So he told me about his sex life, and his friends' sex lives – showing a complete lack of boundaries or standards, in what to talk about. As he said: 'I called to get cheered up.' He was depressed. He self-medicated with alcohol instead of anti-depressants, remaining a mental mess.

One of the girlfriends he talked about, that I was supposed to give HIM sympathy about, was the same woman he had an affair with 25 years before, which he threw in my mother's face. Just, appalling behavior, but he could never see it, because he was just doing what made HIM feel BETTER."

# # #

EXAMPLE:

"One Christmas, when I was still underage as far as drinking went, my father gave me a bottle of expensive tequila as my Christmas present. He wanted to make me into his drinking buddy, as that was how he spent his evenings at home."

# # #

EXAMPLE:

One father, after he'd had a couple of glasses of wine, would start to be negative and say nasty things about all the people he worked with – and anybody he knew. But he was particularly insulting to one of his sons. He told him how he couldn't write at all – and he had just gotten a letter to the Editor accepted and published in a major metropolitan newspaper, and a small sporting newspaper took an article – so the young man WAS a good writer. The father just wanted to make his son feel diminished. The father went out of his way to cruelly LIE, to make his son feel bad. And when the son's new girlfriend came to the house to be introduced, the first thing out of the father's mouth was a cruel put-down: "He doesn't have a job." The son was between jobs at that time because he had just quite working with his toxic father.

\# \# \#

EXAMPLE:

One holiday, a grandfather snuck down the hall into his little granddaughter's bedroom with his camera. He had already several times, threatened to "spank her bare bottom." She was getting so alarmed, that in a restaurant bathroom when her mother was trying to help her dry off in the bathroom stall, the child started yelling: "Don't you touch my bottom! Don't you touch my bottom!"

When he came out of the little girl's slightly messy bedroom, his adult daughter asked what he was doing, and he said he was taking photos of the little girl's room. He smiled gleefully and said: 'I'll use these on her when she's a little older!' He was obviously looking forward to humiliating her.

# # #

EXAMPLE:

Ellie was a lovely woman, who had had an unsuccessful marriage, but had a wonderful relationship with her grown son from the failed marriage. All her boyfriends treated her badly, and dropped her, eventually. She chose very CRUEL men.

She said that when she was a little girl, every morning, at the breakfast table, her father would smile nastily, and say "You're adopted you know." She would protest and cry – and he laughed and laughed at the distress he caused.

# # #

EXAMPLE:

The actor Eric Roberts and the actress Julia Roberts, were both subjected to abuse in the form of violent rages and being hit and having things thrown at them, by their alcoholic stepfather Michael Motes. Since divorcing their mother, he has come out as gay, and lives with his homosexual partner.

Eric Roberts said of him: "It was common knowledge where we grew up that Motes was a freak. He would have stood out in a crowd of ten thousand. Whether he married my mother to get close to her children or not, I don't know. But clearly, marrying him was not a good decision or a healthy thing for her children. Our

Mother's husband terrorized and abused me, and I fear he terrorized my sisters, Julia and Lisa, as well."

# # #

EXAMPLE:

One mother used to swear under her breath when she burned herself cooking, or when she was angry. One evening when her five year old daughter was watching the Mickey Mouse Club show on television, the mother heard the little girl say the word "damn" – a word the mother often said. The mother told the little girl she wasn't to use such a word. When the mother was leaving the living room, the little girl whispered the word "damn" again. The mother flew into a rage and dragged her into the bathroom and jammed a bar of soap in her mouth and said she had to have her mouth washed out with soap for using a dirty word.

# # #

EXAMPLE:

One older, near menopause-age mother of seven children, thought she might have a cyst in her womb when she felt a bump, so she went to the doctor. It turned out that she was pregnant again.

She had the baby, a girl, and then promptly had a nervous breakdown. The baby was raised by two older teenage sisters, in between their attending high school, so the baby was ignored a lot of the time.

The little girl grew up to be a fast swimmer and entered competitions. Her father was a very cruel man, and *"secret" drinker. He came to one swim meet where the young girl had lost first place – come in second – by a quarter of a second.*

Her father then began to berate and insult her publicly at the swim meet about how coming in second was worth NOTHING and how she was a total loser.

Not surprisingly, the girl grew up to trust no one, and be very manipulative, which destroyed a lot of her friendships and ruined her love life. There has to be trust for there to be intimate love – and her father had destroyed her ability to trust.

# # #

EXAMPLE:

One little 3-year old was playing in the tiny house where she lived, and decided to sneak the wooden cooking spoon out of the kitchen that her mother used to hit her with to "punish" her for anything she did "wrong". Later that day, the mother couldn't find the wooden spoon, and intimidated the little girl into pulling it out of where she had hidden it, in the vacuum cleaner cardboard box of attachments. Then the mother started to hit the little girl with the wooden spoon a couple of times to "punish" her for hiding the instrument of torture – the wooden spoon.

# # #

EXAMPLE:

A young father thought he was being extremely funny, when he sitting on his deck watching his 2 young toddler boys play, while he was on his third can of beer, and he decided to start pouring beer down the throats of the little boys. They drank it.

The father laughed uproariously. Then he got the idea of putting his pipe – he smoked constantly – in each of their mouths and making them puff on it until they got into horrible coughing spells.

He was enormously amused. It was like watching some dumb adolescent give beer to his pet dog.

# # #

EXAMPLE:

Jada grew up in a very wealthy Beverly Hills home, where her Hollywood producer father, would sexually molest her at night, several times a week, starting from the age of 6, on. He didn't use threats to keep it secret, as much as bribes.

She was a ten year old wearing a $5,000 tennis bracelet to school, as part of keeping "their secret". He would buy her any clothes she wanted, and she started choosing expensive things to "make him pay" for what she hated doing. She had lots of adult designer clothes, in petite sizes, so they fit her. She had her own subscription to Vogue magazine, and saved all the back issues in her walk-in closet, possibly planning what she would ask him to buy her next.

One day the Latina maid had been cleaning up and had tossed some of the oldest issues of Jada's Vogue magazines in the trash, without asking Jada.

When Jada discovered this, she came down into the kitchen where the maid was washing something in the sink, and Jada took one of her hands, and put it in the garbage disposal, and turned it on.

If adults where going to do mean things to her, Jada was going to do mean things back to them.

# # #

EXAMPLE:

A New York City, a 10-year-old youngster with a deep voice for a child, and good acting skills, was chosen out of a summer school program to go to an "enrichment" class, where she had some one-on-one acting lessons with a very famous star of stage and screen. This very famous woman was as famous as Marilyn Monroe, only was respected for being an excellent actress on Broadway, as well as films. A man who married her made a witty line famous when he met the beautiful actress at a party and handed her some peanuts, and said something like: I wish they were diamonds or emeralds.

The young girl was very excited, until she went for the first of her special lessons. The first one felt very awkward, because it clearly involved this famous female star sexually molesting the 10-year old girl. It may have been done to the "star" herself in the casting couch business of acting – but she molested a 10-year old girl, and got away with it. There probably had been other little girls that she sexually molested since pederasts rarely stop abusing, and no one dared tell on someone so "famous".

# # #

EXAMPLE:

The press released in a May 12. 2014 publication, news of a lawsuit being brought by a young man who stated her was sexually molested and raped when he was 15, by a Hollywood director, Bryan Singer. The young man said that at the time, he and some other kids went to the party hoping to get small parts in movies. The party had a lot of drugs and famous Hollywood actors and directors present, who were using the underage kids like sexual prostitutes, only not paying them – just promising them that they would get a part as an "extra" in a movie. The other abusers who were present, were named in the law suit, but not reported in the article, except to be referred to as: "a former Bond girl, an Irish-born heartthrob, an iconic action star…" and descriptions of that sort.

This lawsuit has termed the abuse actions as part of a "sex ring" designed for established Hollywood stars to prey on underage kids who were desperate to get jobs in the acting business.

# # #

EXAMPLE:

A news publication reported in the May 12, 2014 issue, that on April 1, 2014, a McCandless, PA mother, drowned her 6 year old and 3 year old sons in her bathtub at her home. She claimed she heard "voices" to push them underwater. Laurel Schlemmer, who quit her job as a teacher when she got married, was reported by her Christian minister who married her, as a very "strong Christian". She said she thought the two boys "…would be better off in heaven."

Her oldest boy, was 7, and was on a school bus going to school, when the woman killed the two youngest boys.

She had done other tell-tale questionable acts of violence, but no one intervened. First, in 2009, she had left a toddler unattended in a closed car in a parking lot, that was 112 degrees. She was let off with a reprimand.

Ten months ago, the 3 and 6 year old – who were even younger then – were in the driveway of their house, and their mother backed her van into them both. One child had internal injuries and the other was unable to walk for a period of time.

She has been charged with criminal homicide and other charges, and is in jail, without bond.

# # #

EXAMPLE:

Movie star actor Kirk Douglas, was famous in his time in the spotlight, for being "macho" – playing the part of strong-man Spartacus – and other tough-guy roles. He was questioned in a girlfriend's strange death, but eluded being blamed because he was such a big star at the time. But his ex-wives and sons said that he regularly beat his youngest son, weekly, as hard as he could, to discourage what he thought were "gay" tendencies.

The boy did turn out to be gay. And since his father had abused him for years, it was not surprising that he sought comfort in drugs and alcohol, which eventually killed him.

His surviving brother actor Michael Douglas earned an Emmy Award for his portrayal of gay icon Liberace – which may have been his way of trying to make it up to the little brother he couldn't protect from his abusive father.

# # #

EXAMPLE:

In a national news publication, in the issue for May 12, 2014, was a news story about Jodi Parrack. She was 11 years old when she was found murdered in a cemetery. Recently there was enough evidence to arrest the family friend Raymond McCann, who murdered her. At that time he was a reserve police officer, and was able to redirect the search for her at the time, to delay the discovery of her body.

# # #

EXAMPLE:

"When my mother got cancer, she asked my father to (1) stop smoking in the house – which he refused to do – and (2) she said she needed 'more' from him. He said to her that he had given all he had to give.

My father earned a LOT of money. But he didn't want to spend it on nurses. He didn't care if his children were in serious depression and distress over their mother dying, and he didn't care if their grades dropped, from doing ALL the work that a professional nurse would do. Having her children be cleaning her, calling the ambulance at different times – he didn't care.

She tried to hang on, and went through horrible treatments, and had a few remissions, with her entire focus being living as long as she could to be a buffer between our father and us, so we got hit less often. She wasn't able to stop his verbal insults but she spared us from a lot.

Nevertheless, as soon as my brothers and I got our learner permits to drive, we were driving her to chemotherapy. And one brother had to drive her to a crematorium, at age 16, while she arranged for her own cremation.

My father was no use at all. We didn't get any counseling. Dad just kept drinking so HE was feeling little pain, or at least stuffing it inside.

When she finally died, he didn't sort her things, but asked a neighbor woman to do it. He also didn't call our older brother to tell him when she died. He called his parents, and had his father call our big brother. Later that night our grandfather had his third massive heart attack, from the strain. But my father didn't carry any of the heavy end of the load, at any time.

He also told us not to grieve, because it clearly depressed him.

So I drank a lot, and barely escaped DUIs as a college student. My big brother arranged for us to go sky-diving several times, so we could have some thrill hormones to off-set our depression.

A friend of mine's father, took her to the local hospital where they had counseling for families with cancer. She was told that 'the cancer is your mother's illness – not yours – it should not define your life…' which I thought was really cool."

# # #

EXAMPLE:

A father was very obsessed with money. When his wife was ill, he was secretly looking forward to having control over all their assets, and he expected to inherit money from her wealthy father when he died. Apparently the wife had told her father in a phone conversation how bad things were, and the grandfather's will left nothing to the husband, and divided some money among his daughter's children. This husband was very surprised, and really angry, and also delusional. He said: "The money is supposed to go to the husband." He acted like he'd been cheated, when her father died and left him nothing. It hadn't occurred to him to figure that once she died, all bets were off.

He was a very angry man. His father had beaten him a lot, and when his father died, he told his brother that he had hated him. The two subsequent wives that he married, divorced him, and while he hated both of them too, they also hated him. Money was all he had faith in.

He decided not to pay any money for his children's college education. He spent his money on cruises, and tennis camp trips, and expensive country club memberships, that were just for him, not his children. He got "even" with them for not getting the money that he delusionally thought he would get.

He kept DEDUCTING as dependents, three of his kids, 5 years after they had moved out of the house. This a man who ENJOYED cheating on his income taxes. He looked forward to audits as if they were chances for him to OUTSMART the IRS. Everything was a game to him, to get more money.

# # #

EXAMPLE:

Sexually abused.

"My aunt was a single mother with two daughters, and the youngest daughter was both extraordinarily beautiful, and very manipulative. My aunt had very little money and decided to play into her daughter's manipulation traits. She told her how she could attract men, and let them feel her up, and they would give her money and expensive presents. The daughter did this from age 13 to age 16, and would turn over part of the money or 'presents' to her mother. Then the girl attracted a very wealthy married man, whose family owned the largest jewelry store in the city. The daughter had the man sexually enthralled and her gave her thousands and thousands of dollars of expensive jewelry, which she split with her mother. Finally, he asked her to meet him one evening on the steps of the public library, long after it had closed, and there he shot her. He put a dozen red roses by her corpse. And then he turned the gun on himself and committed suicide."

# # #

EXAMPLE:

Sexually abused by her mother's boyfriend.

"My mother was ineffectual at almost everything, except using her very large bosom to attract men. She could attract a man, and keep him for almost a year, but that was usually the limit. When I was in my pre-teens, she had a boyfriend who brought home a good paycheck, and she was interested in keeping him. When

he started visiting my room at night, I told myself that (1) we needed his income and (2) nobody else in the family was going to save me, and (3) I didn't want my little sister to have to be screwed by him. My brothers were too young to be of any use."

This woman grew up to hate men, and having sex. She had her husband's pet neutered, without asking. She was vicious.

She became a doctor, and caused one man a heart attack, when she declined to pass him as having a mild heart condition – she exaggerated the report – just to show her power and spite him. She was about to be investigated for malpractice, so had a male friend wear a white coat at the hospital, and sneak in and take the file and destroyed the records. She kept on getting revenge for the rest of her life. She had been used like a "prisoner" when she was a child, so as an adult, SHE took prisoners – patients.

# # #

EXAMPLE:

A widowed Borderline Personality disordered man lied to his fiancé about how his kids needed a mother, when really, as he told the teens, he was marrying her because she was "rich", which was what she had pretended. He lied a lot, and he drank a lot, and he refused to take the anti-depressants that a physician prescribed for him, so he took his irritability and depression out on everyone. He traveled a lot for his job so his kids were going to be facing his new wife alone most of the time.

His wife was also a Borderline personality, and was deeply in debt (she had lied about being rich). When he found out she wasn't rich, he traveled more, and she got enraged. She got even by trying to kill 2 of his teen children, once by letting a rattlesnake loose on the lower floor outside the bedrooms where the two preteens slept.

She also tried to starve the 11 year old child. The story of her life had been that her husband had been domestically abusive – he never let her use the checkbook or anything – so she was very calm (maybe happy?) when her first husband died in a plane crash. There was also a story that her 4th child died of Sudden Infant Death Syndrome. But knowing what Emergency medical Technicians now know, there are often signs of children being smothered deliberately, that are then labeled SIDS. The step-kids figured she probably smothered the baby, just to get even. She seemed to LOVE to get even with the men she married.

The step-kids were too afraid of him to tell their father what she did, since he was alcoholic and gone so much traveling, he didn't protect them. They each made plans to run away as soon as they could.

# # #

EXAMPLE:

One 17 year old, was very depressed when his mother died, and his alcoholic father told him to snap out of it, and to NOT do any mourning, while the father was contentedly getting plastered every night for HIS comfort.

The kid took to riding his motorcycle at breakneck speeds in the university district, where he was freshman, after getting drunk.

He would go to Canada and with fake ID, buy brandy bottles, and stuff them inside the hubcaps of his car, and return to the states with them.

Finally, one Friday night, he passed out on the university library steps and was taken to the university hospital for alcohol poisoning. The father was called, and showed up. Two friends of the young man, read the father the riot act and said he was a lousy person and a terrible father, to not help his son get through such a painful time. The drunken father was ASTOUNDED that anyone would try to penetrate his numbed-out haze and tell him off.

# # #

EXAMPLE:

"He told me how his father had beaten him so many times, and so viciously, that he thought he wanted to kill his father. And as he was getting bigger at age 16, he thought that he might lose his self-restraint and actually DO it, and then he'd be in jail and his own life ruined. He had been on the swim team at his upstate New York public school, and he started going to the YMCA and taking scuba diving instruction, and qualified on the level necessary for employment. Then he ran away, and lied about his age. He ended up working for PEMCO in the Gulf of Mexico, repairing oil rigs, underwater. "

# # #

[NOTE: Since 1 in 6 children in America is hungry and not fed enough, many kids have to wait until they are old enough to join the military, to survive, and this young man was rare, in that he had a skill.]

EXAMPLE:

"Soon after my parents divorced, my mother decided to 'show him' – my father – by suddenly deciding to move us 4 states away, almost overnight. I came home from school on a Friday, and over the weekend we moved. My mother had found herself a boyfriend. A big guy who drank. And soon my sister and were in entirely new schools, with no friends, and nobody in the community as extended family or support. I didn't know it until it was diagnosed in later years, that the shock of all that caused me to have Post Traumatic Stress Disorder, as a kid.

Her boyfriend or my 'stepfather' had a few drinking buddies but they didn't come to the house, since my mother ruled the house, making it into a little jewel-box setting for herself. She would actually hold tea parties for new women she wanted to impress.

And she wanted to impress people telling them how smart and talented her children were- all to reflect glory back upon her.

When my stepfather started sexually molesting me, I didn't dare tell her. She never wanted to face any real problems, just problems like what she would fix for an impressive menu.

Her boyfriend drank, outright, but my mother was a secret drinker. She was still a full-blown alcoholic.

Initially I stayed living at home because I felt I could protect my younger sister from my stepfather and I DID succeed at that.

My sister had a much more normal life than I did. Although she did marry a closeted homosexual – or bi-sexual – which I think she did because he was a very weak person and she felt she should protect him. Since I was always protecting our mother – and my stepfather by my silence – she got the overt and unspoken message to be a caretaker. But she did go on to a second marriage that seems okay.

I just don't know where I'm supposed to dump all this ugly junk from childhood."

# # #

[TIP: Telephone help lines can be a wonderful way to UNLOAD, and the people who staff the phones, are trained.]

EXAMPLE:

"My father had these wacky religious beliefs that made him feel 'right' when he beat the crap out of us. He worked at a steel mill and was very strong, and he slapped or punched each of us boys, almost every night.

I saw my father use my mother so badly, that I feared I might have some of that nature in me. So I was a bachelor and able to keep all my relationships friendly, and on the surface. I finally ran away from home, but still lived in the same city. Sometimes I would see one of my brothers or sisters from a distance, but I didn't go talk to them.

My youngest brother was literally a captive, by guilt and false duty, to that power-hungry old man. Finally the old man got sick, and my brother started looking around for someone to marry so he'd have an excuse to get out. Too bad about my sisters, he figured, since he'd been working from age 16 through age 26 bringing home money for them all. Now they could look to their own devices.

I may have escaped earlier than he did, but we were both deeply scarred by being so disrespected and manipulated. I would occasionally see him around town, and we would talk very briefly – and rarely. I think he and I never forgave the old man for his cruelty."

# # #

EXAMPLE:

"My mother had earned a scholarship to work in a chemical lab, which was her dream. Her alcoholic father, with 5 other kids at home, was forcing them all to get work, to support him and his wife, so he didn't have to be a shoemaker anymore. He forced my mother to get a job on an auto plant assembly line because it paid most.

My father walked out on my mother. My mother had never liked men much after her alcoholic father used to hit all her siblings and her. She hated men now more than ever, when her father had been a mean alcoholic, and now she had been abandoned with 2 small boys. When she was angry at us she would throw heavy crockery plates at our heads, when we were in the kitchen. We learned to duck. The plaster wall was nicked with a dozen 'plate marks'.

My mother married again later in life, and was vicious to her second husband's adult daughters, refusing to allow them to visit him – being as mean as possible to off-load her rage.

When her husband had a stroke and needed care, even though they had lots of money, she didn't want to spend it on HIM – a man. So she neglected him. I think she actually killed him, by giving him food too coarse to chew and swallow."

# # #

EXAMPLE:

"I would soothe my father when he was upset, and he called every weekend starting when I was 17, which was strip-mining ME – since he needed a weekly transfusion. Since he REFUSED to take the anti-depressants the M.D. had prescribed for him, he continued to self-medicate with alcohol. When he'd been drinking he would rip into me and criticize me about things I didn't even do – and make demands that were out of line too. If he could play in the country club tennis competitions and win, then he was strong enough to empty his own storage shed and put the boxes into his car and move them himself. But he wanted a 'slave' for it and made me do it – and he expected that his children were his slaves. One of my brothers had been forced to move him once, too, without any reciprocity. Even though I was a 'girl', and even though I had had a back operation, he expected to use me. Which I'm sure he conveniently forgot."

# # #

EXAMPLE:

When she was only 17, her father had decided not to pay for nursing help for her depressed mother, although he had a powerful, good paying job, and made his only daughter drop out of college to take care of her mother when her mother was diagnosed as clinically depressed. Perhaps her mother was so depressed, because she was living with an alcoholic Borderline husband.

The daughter gained 150 pounds that she couldn't seem to lose. Maybe she (1) ate to stuff down her anger and rage at him for manipulating her, or (2) maybe she over-ate to build a wall to be able to repel him in some way since he was such an invasive person.

# # #

EXAMPLE:

In a Boston family with 6 kids, and a dead father, the kids had to help the mother – in addition to the insurance money she had – to meet her expenses. Some of the kids were particularly resentful, and there was SIBLING ABUSE on the youngest kid.

The youngest child, a girl, at age 16, had just won a scholarship to Harvard. At the end of her freshman year, her jealous older brother threatened her that her mother would die if she didn't drop out and come home and take care of her. Then after a few months, when she was already doing all the cooking for her mother, her brother wanted to humiliate her more, and suggested that they save money on a cleaning woman, and that SHE should do it, since she had nothing else to do.

# # #

EXAMPLE:

One young man was beaten so badly by his very strong father, and every other night, that he lied about his age and ran off an enlisted in the navy. Since home life had been terrible, he had been already drinking since he was 14, on the side. Naturally he never had good grades in high school, since he was usually hungover.

In the navy he continued to take risks, because of the alcoholism, started by the beatings at home. Being very impulsive, and being such a regular drinker, he greatly enjoyed taking his turn to slide under the chain link fence of the naval dock compound, and sneak into town and buy liquor, and then return, go back under the fence, and sneak the liquor in to his bunk mates. He loved breaking rules.

# # #

EXAMPLE:

"My father had put me down in all sorts of ways when I was younger. He was deliberately cruel when he needed to feel POWERFUL, like when I was by the beach, he told me I had a big butt. He also said I'd never be a model, or an actress. Years later, I was both a model in national magazines, and had had a few parts on New York soap operas. But what really was crushing was when he put me down for not being smart in school, belittling my ambitions to graduate early, and finish college.

I finally graduated college, then got a masters in graduate school, then did post-graduate work at an Ivy League school.

I had to label all the 'bad stuff' as LIES, so I could then ignore what he said to me. He was just trying to make me as small as possible, so he was not upstaged."

# # #

EXAMPLE:

Walt Disney had a rough childhood with a harsh father.

Walt Disney and his brother Roy were used as free labor by their father, who distributed a newspaper, twice a day. They lived in a cold climate in the winter, which Disney recalled could have 4 foot drifts of snow. The boys were sent out in the morning before school to deliver papers – on foot – getting totally frozen and wet, and then they'd come home and change and go to school. Walt Disney said he was too exhausted to ever pay attention in school.

Then in the afternoon they had to go deliver the evening edition, and became soaked and frozen again. They'd get dried off and put to bed, and the whole nightmare would begin again the next day. And if he DIDN'T deliver every paper, his father would beat him with a belt.

Walt Disney chose to use those experiences as the basis of his optimistic view of childhood – trying to INSTILL HOPE in many of his creations.

# # #

Celebrities are not people who were "lucky" to escape child abuse or neglect. Many times they are people who triumphed despite being abused or neglected. The famous comedienne

Carole Burnett, grew up in poverty with her grandmother taking care of her, while her alcoholic mother drank. Out of a tragic childhood – just like Charlie Chaplin – she forged a career and glittering life, giving people the <u>release</u> and <u>joy</u> of <u>laughter</u>.

EXAMPLE:

Famous film actor and former Saturday Night live comic, Chevy Chase, grew up in financial comfort, with a lovely home and money for special schooling, but he was regularly beaten by his parents. He turned his back on his childhood abuse and pain, and also gave others the gift of laughter, in his comic antics, and hopefully found some healing in his talents.

# # #

EXAMPLE:

Academy Award winning actress Charlize Theron was born and raised on a farm in South Africa in a household of severe domestic violence, which is abusive to the child, even if they are "only" witnesses to what happens to their parent. Finally, one time when her father had a gun and threatened to kill Charlize's mother and Charlize, her mother used a different gun, and shot him to death. After working hard as an adult to create the life she has, she was recently quoted about her life: "I have nothing to complain about. I'd be a disgrace to humanity if I had anything to complain about. Life has been very good."

# # #

EXAMPLE:

In April, 2014, the television actor and former "Shield" show star, Michael Jace, murdered his wife, April, in front of their children. Her job didn't pay enough to support them both, and after his television show went off the air, they had severe money problems. And they argued about their financial pressures.

# # #

EXAMPLE:

In May, 2014, two famous movie star millionaire parents, Will Smith and Jada Smith, were the subject of a Los Angeles County Department of Children and Family Services investigation, of being neglectful parents. An anonymous complaint was made to LA County with a photo that had been posted on the Internet, of their 13 year old daughter reclining, clothed, on a bed with a 20-year old male, prompted concerns. Obviously the daughter wanted more attention from her parents, or she would not have posted the photo – now removed. The parents said that they knew the boy and that there was nothing sexual about the situation.

# # #

EXAMPLE:

In May, 2014, former Baywatch television show actress, and film star, Pamela Anderson, announced her foundation charity for animal rights. As she spoke, she told the world's press about her child abuse, which she had never told her parents about. A news publication quoted her: "Despite having loving parents, I was molested from age 6 to 10 by my female baby sitter. I kept these events to myself."

She reported that she was raped by a 25 year old man when she was 12, and that her boyfriend arranged for her to be gang-raped when she was in her first year of high school. She said: "I wanted off this Earth."

Her family was devastated when they learned about this. Her parents had been working all her childhood, and had been dependent upon outside child care for her and her younger brother, who could not protect her. She said: "Sometimes when you smile, it's not because (you are) happy. It's because you are strong."

Her efforts to protect animals from cruel treatment, is the work of a strong person, who survived and transcended her injuries.

# # #

EXAMPLE:

"This woman Noreen was my stepmother, and had come from grinding poverty in Maine. She and her sister never had a doll, they were so poor. Her father was a mill worker, did domestic violence at home, and drank away any money he earned. The family had to ask the local Catholic church for hand-outs. Noreen married a first husband, who drank way, way too much, and finally suicided one day, in his home office.

Noreen stayed in denial much of her life, after growing up abused. She would say like the movie heroine

Scarlett O'Hara "I'll think about that tomorrow". Only she never did think about things.

She married a second husband who had been an alcoholic for 50 years. Her son couldn't stick to any part-time job, or do well at school. Starting in his teens, he was drinking on the side a lot of the time. She turned a blind eye to – and actually CAUSED A LOT OF HIS UNHAPPINESS. She was verbally vicious to people who did not compliment her enough. She required constant admiration, leaving others like a wrung-out sponge. She used to brag about her handsome son, but then she turned on him, saying he was worthless. He finally found a therapist to help him.

I watched her make a Bloody Mary for her son when he was visiting one weekend that I was visiting, and it was barely 10:30 in the morning. I think she was a co-dependent who liked all the men in her life controllable – so if someone was a little – or a lot – drunk – she was even more in charge."

# # #

EXAMPLE:

Killing his former wife and kids.

Gerald Uden pleaded guilty in November, 2013, to killing his former wife and children. One of the motivations for his killing them may have been his NEW wife's constant nagging him about how the alimony and child support for those people "were bleeding them dry" financially. Clearly his NEW wife had no conscience about urging such a drastic act – murder – for her own convenience.

It is said that many serial killers are killing for a sexual thrill, while many female killers are killing to get some <u>financial advantage</u> – perhaps killing their spouses, or "johns" and robbing them, or by reducing their expenses when they kill their children.

# # #

EXAMPLE:

"My father drank a lot when we were growing up in Montana, and since lots of other people around there drank a lot too, no one said much. But my mother began to hate it. Finally, when I was 14, my mother upped and left him. That left ME having to care for 2 younger brothers, and my father.

He got drunker and drunker, and began to sexually molest me. My mother had moved two states away, up near Vancouver, Canada, so that she wouldn't be able to get to us often, and she didn't try to.

In later years, after she had made herself a 'healer' as an herbalist and had a strong enough following to make a living at it, she was happy for me as an adult, to get in touch with her, and we became close. She even expected me to take care of her in her old age, I could tell.

As for my father, at one point, after I had been a doctor for a couple of years, I went and visited him, and just talked a little to see if there was any remorse, or any apology forthcoming, and there wasn't. So I said that I would never talk to him, or see him again. I turned on my heel and left, and I have never followed up on him since. He could be physically dead, and he's certainly emotionally dead to me."

\# \# \#

EXAMPLE:

Crashed a small plane with his daughter in it.

The national news had extensive coverage of this forest ranger who was divorced, and who had become completely enraged over it. He rented a small plane on a weekend he had custody of his young daughter, so he then flew the plane over the countryside to where his mother-in-law lived, and where his ex-wife was supposedly staying that weekend. He crashed the plane into the house. His ex-wife was not there. He killed himself and his young daughter.

\# \# \#

EXAMPLE:

A father killing his young sons in a deliberate house fire.

This news story got national attention in February 2012, because of the gruesome and totally planned nature, of the murders, which occurred in the state of Washington. The father, Josh Powell, had done domestic violence in his home, abusing his wife, and terrifying his young children. His own father, Steve Powell, had been an imprisoned sex offender. He was frustrated about his financial situation, and he didn't think he could continue to afford the house he was in and pay child support. His wife had disappeared, and authorities assume he murdered her. On a weekend when he had custody of his young boys, he shot everyone, put enormous amounts of fire accelerants all around the property, then lit the matches, and then shot himself.

All that was left was a completely blackened piece of ground – all ash.

# # #

EXAMPLE:

Unacknowledged domestic violence

For children, just seeing their parents argue, becomes a hostile environment, and is abusive to the kids. Verbal violence counts as domestic violence, as does slamming doors and throwing things, even if there is not hitting. One ten year old boy was told a lie by his father that he was going off to start a farm and he would come back and get him. By age 11, the little boy felt that he would never have a normal family life again. His younger brother felt equally abandoned, and made up an imaginary friend, and in later life was a raging alcoholic. The mother didn't tell the boys why their father had left. He did send some money to them, and possibly some letters, but the mother was vengeful and never passed any communication on to the boys. When the eldest boy was an adult, and could drive, he looked up his father, once. This type of abandonment is a form of child abuse that is very widespread, but it gets covered up under the label of a "divorce happened to the family." The family was an abusive place for children, long before the abandonment and divorce.

EXAMPLE:

Eleanor thought she had married beneath her social standing, so she had a lot of unrealistic expectations – delusions – about how she should be treated, how much money she be able to spend on things, while her husband earned money working in a shipyard. Her alcoholic father had gone through all his inheritance money, and then all of her mother's inheritance money, leaving Eleanor in very tight financial straits when she was a teen. They had had to sell their summer beach house that the family had owned for 2 generations. Her mother divorced her father, took a job working for the city, and turned their home into a boarding house. Eleanor went from being rich and spoiled, to there not being enough money to send her to college, even though her older sister got to go.

She resented a LOT of things.

Finally, her husband found a friendly lady, and on Saturdays would go visit her, for an affair that lasted a year.

When Eleanor found out, she got her revenge by mentally abusing her two young sons. Each day when they came home from middle school, she would sit them down in the kitchen and tell them for an hour or more, what a terrible person their father was – and it was implied by their being males – that they might turn out badly, too. She totally EXHAUSTED these children, using them for her ADULT problems. Both children were depressed before they even reached high school age, and battled depression, and heavy drinking, all their adult lives.

# # #

[NOTE: There is a lot of research that depressed parents CAUSE childhood depression in their offspring.]

EXAMPLE:

A cruel millionairess mother.

[NOTE: A survey conducted by a U.S. "Shelter" magazine with very rich readers – both the husband and the wife in the average readership family earned $200,000 per year, found that these "status-oriented" mothers wanted: (1) a big house, (2) a husband with a well paying job, and (3) good-looking children. Kids were only "good" if they were GOOD LOOKING.]

Lena was the millionairess widow who fit the mold of the people who took that survey. She had married a man who had made his fortune doing landscaping bids for state highways. She had 3 sons who all worked in the family business, and she made them live with their wives in a compound around her much bigger house.

The setting was beautiful, and had lush landscaping and expensive riding horses.

Lena was smart, articulate, and very, very beautiful. She still had a model's face and figure after 3 children. But from the time they were little boys she had VERBALLY BELITTLED her sons. She had told them for DECADES that they would be NOTHING without her, and that no one else would ever hire them, because they were basically losers.

She was cruel to neighbors too. She taunted one neighbor who lived a few acres away, in a much more modest house – she was a school teacher – by saying: "We should fly to Paris for lunch on my private plane.

Of course, we'll have to split the bill for the fuel." She knew that was just a cruel mockery of the teacher's lack of money, and allowed her to feel SUPERIOR to her.

She was very, very cruel to her son's wives. She had been so mean to the boys for so many decades starting when they were just 6 years old, that they had no psychological backbone to defend their wives. They actually wanted their wives to SHIELD THEM from their monstrous mother.

Lena said, in the hearing of one of her daughters in law, who had a baby in a stroller near her as she was doing some cleaning-up in the tree farm: "...that's her third child...you know that hearty peasant stock – they just pop them out and keep working."

Lena continued to lead the guest on the tour of the tree farm, and the daughter-in- law immediately started up a chain saw to drown out conversation, and take out some of her aggression on the branches of some of the trees on the grounds.

# # #

EXAMPLE:

Joanie was beautiful, blond, and scared, since she had just survived breast cancer reconstruction. She was worried about her youngest boy, who was too young to work at McDonalds' or anywhere. She had little income since each husband she had married had been a "deadbeat".

Joanie, as an 8-year old little girl, had watched her father shoot and murder her mother. She never told. In her life, it was still FAMILIAR to hook up with "bad boys", with the resulting abandonment that inevitably followed. She had not had the financial luxury of being able to do any therapy work to discover her very significant "strengths" as a person.

# # #

EXAMPLE:

"One time when I was 10, my mother went through my bedroom, since I didn't clean it all up by myself at that age, and she found a coin purse. Since I had "borrowed" another girl's doll for more than 2 weeks and had been forced to return it, my mother was afraid I would turn into both a liar and a petty thief, which is what she thought of my father.

He traveled for business and he would bring home all the things you were supposed to LEAVE at the hotel – all the wood hangars and bathrobes. My mother's face would just fall – she looked sickened when she saw his suitcase.

But she knew he was a serious alcoholic and cheater. She found out about the affairs. The alcoholism was apparent when he threw up on the dance floor at his own accounting company's annual Christmas party. She was the one who wiped up the vomit.

So she thought I was lying when I said that SHE gave me the coin purse. I couldn't remember where it came from. She resorted to child abuse.

She screamed: "Don't you lie to me!" over and over. I think she was really screaming at my dad, in her head.

So she kept slapping my face and my head whipped back and forth and tears were pouring down my face because I really DID think she had given it to me.

Hours later I remembered that her husband's mother had given it to me – it had come with a new handbag she bought.

The scary thing was how this set me up to tolerate – and expect that it would happen to me – future abuse.

At a date when I was 17, a girl I didn't know who was drunk, pushed out of the crowd in the darkness at the edge of a patio, and slapped me as hard as she could across the face.

This was supposedly for me not liking my best friend's brother, who liked me. Like that was HER business! Maybe she was jealous for misplaced reasons.

But (1) I didn't cry, (2) didn't report her to my host, (3) I didn't call the police for an assault, and when I got back to school, (4) I didn't tell a counselor.

I expected to be treated shitty, I guess."

# # #

EXAMPLE:

I heard this man in a court-mandated domestic violence skills training class. He was talking about his childhood and started to cry, when he recounted, when he was only 8, how some older boys made him help them kill some kittens that had been abandoned in the woods.

His sensitivity, and conscience were still there, after decades. But his childhood life left no time for him to gather skills from observing competent caregivers – since he was forced to be the caregiver. He had to stand on a stool to reach the stove, and scrounge some canned food to open and cook for his two younger siblings, every night, and then put them bed. He had to force himself to stay awake when he wanted to doze off, because it was his assignment to walk down 5 blocks in the dark at near midnight, to retrieve his drunken mother and father and walk them home. They didn't have drivers licenses anymore. Although they may have been useless most of the time as parents, there was NO ONE ELSE there for him and his siblings.

He was exhausted every day so of course he didn't pay attention well in school and got terrible grades. He was very smart, had an excellent memory, and had done well in the Army. He was only able to get work as a roofer – highly dangerous – but frequently needed, so he could earn money for his own young family.

# # #

EXAMPLE:

A father who had a powerful job running a television station in a top-ten market, was known to be a terror to work for he was so demanding. At his home, he was not much better. His wife admitted that she had never divorced him, because she liked the status in the community that his job provided. And she had never protected her daughter, because she didn't want her husband to get angry at her, and possibly dump her.

So, every other night, when his teenage daughter took a bath, she was forced to leave the bathroom door open 6 *inches – she was <u>forbidden</u> from locking the door – and her father would spy on her nude, adolescent body.*

He was cruel and with-holding, to the very end, when he had an early heart attack and died.

The daughter's first marriage degraded into divorce, but she was an excellent mother to her young son, and was hoping to jump-start a career in one of the recovery professions.

She grew up to be very smart, and very sad, and on anti-depressants. Her father had never even given her a summer intern job, even though she had earned a college degree in communications, and had a great face and voice for broadcasting. She was made to feel inadequate and not good enough, for decades. Her mother was later very, very sorry and apologetic. She could not, however, roll back the clock, nor undo her lack of protection.

# # #

EXAMPLE:

One man became an M.D. psychiatrist and worked with people who had survived childhood abuse. He even worked with murderers in prison. He found that two years of medication to change their habitual fear and aggression reactions, could calm them down enough, to get through 3 times a week skills training, to learn how to be regular adults. They actually could become functioning in society.

The doctor had been a quiet, overweight child, with a deep love of books, and did very well in school, and was loved a lot, and then his father died. His mother remarried a stepfather in the building business. This man was deliberately cruel.

He forced the overweight, not physically fit adolescent, to work like a slave, for free, for his construction business in the heat of summer. He made the kid pour tar over roof shingles, getting burned many times, and made him climb ladders carrying things far too heavy for him – all to "make a man out of him!" as the mean stepfather would yell. His mother wanted to stay married, so she did not overtly protect her son.

# # #

EXAMPLE:

One mother was walking late at night, home from a distant grocery store where she had picked up a bottle of milk, and she was walking her 6 year old daughter with her. They had to cross a railroad track to continue on the road that would take them home.

When the train whistle blew, announcing that it would be rushing over the tracks really soon – the mother did not pick up her daughter and carry her, but dragged her – the child holding on in a death grip, terrified they would be killed by the train – as the mother raced to run over the tracks before the train got there – for the mother's OWN excitement. The child was absolutely terrified. The mother wanted excitement.

# # #

[Many parents give no consideration to the difference in proportion in how kids react, versus adults, to frightening events.]

EXAMPLE:

One young father had been drinking daily since he was 13 or 14 years old, on the sly, and once he got his own house, wife, and little baby girl, he set about making beer in the basement at night – his idea of perfect happiness.

His wife, who had had to give up her managerial job at the same company, in order to get him hired, was disgusted. They had lots and lots of fights. The little girl developed night terrors. She was so frightened so much of the time, that she developed a shortage of GABA – which regulates the body during sleep – and when there's a shortage, a person sleepwalks.

The frightened little 3 year old would walk the halls almost every night. One night she even unpacked some groceries left in a bag on the kitchen floor, and the parents thought there was a burglar in the house.

The mother wanted a divorce. The overly aggressive – and usually slightly drunk – husband threatened her that he would see that child "Cut in half before I will let you have her!" So the child was threatened with being hurt or killed, and the father's violence was making life ever more frightening in that house, and divorce and escape seemed a distant dream.

That childhood fear, for the little girl, resulted in permanent sleep problems, with nightmares for 20 years, until some good therapist helped removed the biggest, worst ones. She was also damaged by being left with a traumatic memory – sometimes called a "flash" memory' – out of so often being in "alarm" mode – watching for the next threat. She had a very bad case of Post Traumatic Stress Disorder for more than 40 years.

# # #

EXAMPLE:

One woman's mother and father began to have vicious fights, as the kids were emerging from childhood into adolescence, and the mother wanted more opportunities for the kids.

The father worked for the Justice Department in Washington D.C., and he pulled some strings, and got his wife committed to a mental hospital. His children were terrified, for their mother, and for what he might to do to them in the future.

The oldest was an 11 year old girl, who began acting like the "mother" in the house. Home was such a potentially frightening place – you could be removed from it, you could die from living in it, that the girl started carefully eavesdropping on her father's phone calls at home, hoping to not be surprised. Eventually the mother was released, but she became physically ill from all the stress and died. Then the father brought home a new "wife" who was only 5 years older than his oldest child.

The oldest child, the girl, grew up feeling very, very insecure. She never got over her mistrust of people. She would eavesdrop on telephone conversations, that she would force her children to have. The phone would ring – she would make one of her kids pick up the phone – and she would listen on the extension. If it was something she wanted to do or was interested in, she would sometimes break into the conversation.

She had been used terribly, and had no idea what was "normal" and could not avoid using her own kids.

# # #

EXAMPLE:

One father got very impatient with his son and daughter over their affection for their cat. They had raised it from being a kitten, and had it a couple of years, and he might have been jealous of how much they LOVED the cat, versus being affectionate to him. (Many abused kids find the family pets are the greatest source of affection in their households.) He was the kind of man who would say: "I want my kids to look up to me." He seemed to want the admiration and affection, without doing anything to earn it.

One day when the kids were at school, he took the cat to the animal pound. When they came home, he told them the cat was gone, and was never coming back, and they would never be having a pet again, in HIS house.

The trauma of loss was severe. The little boy developed vision problems – possibly he didn't want to psychologically "see" what was happening at his house. The little girl started having extremely painful headaches. Stress can cause severe headaches, even in children, and again, children often love their pets – and their siblings – more than the abusive adults in their lives – so the loss is very great.

# # #

EXAMPLE:

One mother was very beautiful, and had three daughters, all of whom she was more beautiful than – which was probably fortunate. Their father was smart, and emphasized that they do well in school, which they did, so they were eventually able to have careers in their adult lives.

But as children, their beautiful, but slightly mentally ill mother, needed daily temper tantrum releases, and would manufacture instances to have them, in the form of child abuse.

One time she asked her 12 year old daughter, Cleo, to trim her hair for her. She sat down, and told the kid to just go across, 1 inch, and that it would be simple.

The girl did what she was told, but the mother was furious with the minor trim and yelled and screamed hysterically that Cleo has ruined her mother's hair! The father redid the trim, and could honestly find nothing to fix, but kept his mouth shut. The mother had wanted to have her "rage" scene – and she'd had it – to the discomfort of the entire family – which made her feel very much in control.

She went on to demean Cleo in front of her two sisters, saying; "No one really likes Cleo do they? She doesn't have many friends, and probably never will, since she is so unlikeable."

The cruelest form of rejection a parent could do, this woman would do, short of putting a child out on the street.

The mother set up the entire trim experience as a set-up so she could have the "high" and release of blowing up! and when others are afraid of your anger – you have demonstrable power-over them! This mother was mentally ill that way, and their father worked, so he couldn't protect the kids all the time. In the evenings there would be big fights when he would disagree with his wife and stick up for the kids, and the same thing would happen on weekends. It was a war-zone of a house to live in.

# # #

EXAMPLE:

One mother had just had a newborn baby, and three younger children, when her husband was transferred to another city. They had to temporarily rent a house in the university section of the city, while their new house in a subdivision was being finished. The father would work late, and when he was home, he was into his second or third martini, and no help at all.

The mother, one night, when it was pitch dark out, but maybe only 8 o'clock at night, made her oldest child, her 7-year-old daughter, walk 6 blocks to the Safeway grocery store to get some food they needed for dinner. The mother didn't want to "set off" her angry husband. The little girl was scared of the dark, and was terrified that she would be jumped on and mugged for her little $10. grocery money, by some of the drug-users that were on every corner.

A wife who had such problems with her husband, that he wouldn't even help when she had a newborn baby, really needed to get professional outside help, rather than exploiting a terrified little kid.

# # #

EXAMPLE:

One Latino teenage father had promised to marry this lovely non-Latino girl, if she would get pregnant. She had the baby, and then their relationship fell apart. He started stalking her house sometimes. He got weekend visitation rights with the little girl they had, and he "got his revenge" on his former girlfriend, by every time when he had the little girl, he would cut some of her hair off.

He didn't ask. It didn't look pretty.

It was a form of control and mutilation of the child.

# # #

EXAMPLE:

Serena was a beautiful little blond, who one day when she was five, and was playing in the living room with her younger sister, heard a loud noise go off.

Her mother had shot herself, committing suicide in the master bedroom.

For the rest of her life, Serena spoke in a voice that was a near whisper, and loud noises continued to scare her. She had a very severe case of Post Traumatic Stress Disorder, that did not get treated.

Serena's womanizing father very quickly brought home a new wife, who came with her own two children.

The children were so lonely, they sort of fell in love with each other, and had crushes, to get any affection.

The stepmother was very rigid and mean.

On Serena's wedding day, she wanted to spoil it and wanted to diminish and humiliate Serena. She whispered into the beautiful bride's ear: "You know your mother was only an Italian!" Which was intended as a racial slur.

# # #

EXAMPLE:

One young mother was distressed when her lovely cat disappeared off the front porch steps. She thought it had probably been stolen, but she wanted to be sure that it hadn't wandered off. Her husband was too self absorbed and drunk to help her, so she dragged her 5 year old daughter with her, walking over steep hills for almost an hour, calling for the beloved cat. The little girl was so sad that her cat was lost. Calling its name over and over was just further trauma.

The mother could have taken on the responsibility herself, but perhaps she felt that she was doing practically everything in her married life, alone, so she started taking her kids into life as "mini-adults", who were not equipped to deal with the stresses and strains that the mother was wrestling with. Loneliness makes a lot of parents behave in ways that are not good for the children.

It was a night of heartbreaking loss for the little girl. They went home that night after a blazing red-orange sunset. For more than 15 years, the girl couldn't understand why she was so sad and alarmed whenever red sunlight would come in through the window and play on the wall.

It was all part of the traumatic memory of losing the cat she loved and being forced to hopelessly look for it – absorbing her mother's anxiety and grief, and having no help processing her own loss.

# # #

EXAMPLE:

Another example of child abuse, this time of a father's sexual abuse of his daughter, with his wife's knowledge, was published in People magazine in June, 2014. Heather Orr reported that her father had begun sexually abusing her in Ohio when she was very young, and it continued when she was 14. Orr said she told her story publicly for "myself and other sexual abuse victims who have borne their pain silently."

Heather said that at age 14, as soon as she knew what was happening was wrong, and talked to her parents, they said: 'If you tell, you're going to be stuck in foster care, you dad will go to jail, and do you really want to be the cause of all this for something that's really not that bad?" I was a mess.

She told a social worker what happened, and then the family abruptly moved to Arizona where her father continued to sexually abuse her. When she graduated at 16 she moved out. She got her father to briefly go to therapy with her, then he quit going. She got him on tape in a telephone conversation admitting to what he'd done, and she used that to press charges. Then her parents moved and took her younger brother, and she couldn't find them for 12 years.

Heather found her brother through the Internet.

Sgt. Gerard Moretz helped put together the investigation that helped send her father to prison in October 2012. Both parents were found guilty on civil charges of abuse and neglect. He said about Heather: "She's a real inspiration." She finally was reunited with beloved brother. Heather Orr was quoted: "Speaking openly and boldly with our children can save them from abuse. I knew my father's actions were wrong, and I won't ever forget that. But I can forgive him for being human and making a mistake. Forgiveness is not for him but for me, to be able to move on."

# # #

6 – STEPS FOR HEALING

"Enjoy your life's journey. It's later than you think."
Chinese Proverb

Every life has both pain and joy in it, and our human challenge when we have suffered trauma, is to get the TRAUMATIC REACTIONS minimized, so that we can return to a state where we can grow, and love, and more happily live.

An inspiring example is the former television child star actress Mackenzie Phillips, who is now a sober counselor at a Recovery Center, because: "It's time for me to get grateful for what I have and share my recovery with other people."

Her father John Phillips of "The Mamas and the Papas", used to have Mackenzie roll his marijuana joints for him, when she was 10 years old. She went through an amazing 11 rehab experiences to recover from heroin and cocaine addictions, caused by her father's sexual incest of her.

Your own life journey – around the obstacles that may seem like mountains – can be traveled by going <u>around</u> them – not up or through them – and it takes the time it takes – but you can accelerate it by doing all the recovery steps of fast healing trauma.

There is no "one-size-fits-all" solution to getting over trauma, there are many ways to recover. Most of the ways require some form of "self-care" or "re-parenting yourself".

Keep in mind that every single human life has some significant pain in it. As a child you did not have the economic or personal power to choose who would inflict pain on you. As an adult, you DO have a choice who you let hurt you.

If you are in an environment that poses risks of hurting you on any level, get out of that place. You are (1) more capable now, you're ADULT (2) you know other people and you can ASK FOR HELP, (3) as an adult, you may have seen enough miracles to call upon a higher power and have faith that you will get some form of help, (4) you may have felt WEAK when you were little – now you have an ADULT body and are no longer powerless.

You can use your mind, and find resources to help you. Society is different now, and even the fire department accepts newborn babies, and there are 24-hour rescue resources.

The first step to heal people in war trauma, domestic trauma, and childhood trauma, is to be WITNESSED – to be believed that you were unfairly hurt, by an abuser.

Being witnessed – by a counselor, group counseling, a special interest group such as domestic violence or rape counseling – or by a 12-step group – provides a time when a person learns that what happened to them was neglect, or physical abuse, or cruel verbal and psychological abuse – or sexual abuse. With so many abusers blaming the victims, many victims are unsure if they were even abused, when by any standards, they were.

Diagnosing the damage to plan a recovery

After child neglect and abuse has been inflicted, it can be hard to determine the degree of injury at a psychological or physical level. The latest discoveries of injury to the brain from sustained traumatic stress in children, show that a biochemical change takes place, making the cells less full – and less able to transmit at high speeds. Mental abuse literally diminishes mental capacity. It has been long known that a psychological blow – from a verbal insult to the loss of a loved one – does as much physical harm to the body as punching someone in the solar plexus and knocking them down. Researchers now know that there is a chemical change that reduces cell functioning capacity.

Research about abuse shows that:

- Children who have been abused in ANY way – psychological, sexual or physical abuse, or neglect – have a VERY high chance of growing up to have the symptoms and detriments of PTSD – Post Traumatic Stress Disorder. Over 80% of abused children have PTSD, often severely.
- People need time to RECOVER from EVERY sort of injury.

One method of counseling a would-be suicide is to start asking them what completes a life – and when most people in such dire distress answer these questions, they start to think of a person who would help them, who gives them a reason to live. Calm down a person, when hysteria takes over, so that a person can see that there are people who would help him if he asked. Find a reason to hope.

Any trauma destroys trust. It can be watching a pet die – the scale of what is traumatizing is different for children than for adults, but in war or in childhood, all trust is destroyed. Trust drops to zero, and this (1) interferes with learning, (2) interferes with healing recovery, and (3) interferes with love, since learning how to trust appropriately is part of intimate love with another person.

Illnesses caused by neglect and abuse

Dr. Charles Whitfield, an M.D. psychiatrist, has spent decades collating data from all the big research universities on abnormal behaviors, and has concluded that all the studies showed a direct correlation between specific behaviors and specific types of child abuse.

The neglected child – one who is not talked to or touched or hugged – often turns super introvert, and can even register on the autism scale, although they may not have been born autistic at all. The neglected child can also become such an introvert that they become "schizoid" and cut off from their own feelings, as well as any feelings for other people. They become labeled as having Asperger's Syndrome, if their concentration on internal information gathering is still high, while their social skills are low. They can fail to recognize even the most basic of human social cues, so are doomed to loneliness and depression. They don't even know how to do basic eye contact – when their caretakers have been so neglectful as to not have done it with them.

For the kid who was sexually abused or physically hit a lot, it can often happen that the kid grows up to have Borderline Personality Disorder, which is a form of depression and narcissism with lots and lots of anger. These folks have tantrums constantly, and adore doing verbal put-downs of others – making others smaller makes them feel taller. Excessive aggression is a reaction to keep others off of them, after having been abused too much as kids. Their super aggressiveness puts them in the category of a future abuser, themselves. If they are very introverted, but were heavily physically abused, they may develop multiple personality disorder, to cope enough to survive the childhood abuse.

All is not hopeless, as has been learned from studying babies adopted from orphanages. In orphanages the world over, the babies and young children usually test out with some learning disadvantage, or as being behind kids who were raised in secure families and more affection and holding. Do not underestimate the power of positive touch. The good news is that most adopted children catch up after 2-3 years.

As adults, some people can not reveal the extent or type of their damage due to factors such as (1) family roles they played such as "hero" that doesn't admit any flaws, or (2) being born an oldest child role where one is treated like a little adult, or (3) the neglect or abuse is so deeply buried that the person may be unaware of the extent of it.

THE CHALLENGES –

The pain for a child is so different from an adult prisoner of war, because a child did not knowingly put themselves at risk.

Recovery challenges for a child who was neglected or abused are (1) trouble remembering everything clearly from so long ago, (2) having the abuser retell the abuse, maintaining that it didn't happen or it was all in the child's mind, and (3) fear of being punished or injured further, for telling. This can go on for years!

IN THE CASE OF CHILD SEXUAL ABUSE –

Everyone is a unique human being with their own ways of reacting to what happens to them in life.

Some people seem to recover from traumatic events by going ALL THE WAY THROUGH their reactions, and then reduce their emotional triggers so it becomes less.

Others have a memory block. A jogger in Central Park, in the 1990s, who was violently raped, leads a very different life now. Originally severely injured, she eventually recovered, moved to the suburbs, married, still jogs all the time, and her memory does not recall the event at all! The African American teens who were put in prison for that rape, were themselves abused. A tragedy can snowball into several tragedies.

One way that takes energy and commitment, but moves one from victim to survivor mode quickly, is to become an advocate in the arena in which you were hurt. So one woman who was sexually molested as a child by her father, donated many hours of her time to a Domestic Violence center.

EXAMPLE:

Certainly, not every girl in the American South is raped as an adolescent, gets pregnant, has a miscarriage while under 16, and pulls herself together through a school scholarship and a small speaking and beauty contest – and parlays that into the career of billionaire activist and educator, Oprah Winfrey.

Oprah was a dedicated little girl who did very well in school, and was a victim of circumstance by being abused – too many potential predators and too little supervision – which was widespread in poverty stricken areas of the South where both parents worked extra long days. Oprah's mother was a maid – as her mother had been before her –and no one was around to protect little Oprah. There was no money for daycare – there was NO daycare!

Oprah Winfrey, did, however, do the unique act of airing a television special on child sexual abuse and neglect on ALL three major TV channels, NBC, ABC, and CBS, in the 1980s, to educate millions of Americans about what child abuse WAS.

She is an outstanding illustration of the power of taking the way in which one was hurt, and becoming an advocate for others, to remove one's feelings of shame or humiliation, and rightly put them where they belong – on the abuser.

# # #

KEY POINTS –

- Recovery is accelerated by grieving to get the fear hormones and toxins out of the body. It's estimated to take 2,300 hours of crying.
- Join a martial arts group where a guy wears a padded suit, and each woman in the group takes turns to come hit him with a stick as hard as she can.
- Use Emotional Freedom Technique (google EFT exercises), or get EMDR exercise training – both of which toughen the body to lessen the arousal of the bad memory, and lessen the bad memory by putting a NEW message of greater strength and competence, over the old memory.
- Join a group that acts as advocates for kids who have no one standing up for them, such as a family domestic violence group, or Alateen, or a rape crisis clinic.

EXAMPLE:

The child star of "Home Alone", Macaulay Culkin, made a <u>fortune</u> for his family, and his manager father took millions of it, not dividing it up. The adult Macaulay had to sue his father, but did recover much of the funds.

# # #

EXAMPLE:

A young woman was saving money to make a tuition payment, when her bank account was emptied by an attorney collecting money that her PARENTS owed. The financial abuse happened to the daughter – and her only recourse was to have less contact with her parents, who had left her so exposed to the underhanded financial dealings they did.

# # #

EXAMPLE:

On a national level, a 9-11 widow discovered that after 9-11, the U.S. government was giving all the widows and surviving families the run-around, and were under-paying death benefits as assessed by accepted actuarial standards.

Who wants to take on the U.S. Government – who has the time or the will?

Kristen Breitweiser turned to the press and used their extensive resources to "out" the shameful treatment the government was dishing out. She also wrote one of the best of the 9-11 books: "Wake-up Call – the Political Education of a 9-11 Widow." She educated millions of people to the situation, and kicked off a trend of other 9-11 widows writing books.

# # #

KEY POINTS –

- These people examined the wounds that were inflicted upon them, and did their best to recover from them.
- Everyone who has experienced neglect, psychological, sexual or physical abuse, has TRAUMA – which (1) reduces trust in others and yourself and (2) reduces your will. Everyone can benefit from EFT or EMDR exercise training – both of which lessen the bad memory by putting a new message on top.
- The people who healed the most, joined groups that act as advocates for kids who have no one standing up for them, so they became survivors and are no longer victims.

IN THE CASE OF PSYCHOLOGICAL AND EMOTIONAL ABUSE DAMAGE –

As a child, if you were subjected to mean put-downs only twice a day, by the time you left school you could have received over 10,000 CRUEL and DEMEANING messages, all attacking you. You can't resist all these "blows" to your feeling of respect for yourself. This has lasting effects and REDUCES YOUR WILL as an adult.

EXAMPLE:

One young man was over-punished for small infractions, as a rambunctious 3 year old. His dad was an alcoholic with a short-fuse who was usually hung-over and angry. One time, his dad was driving, and had had enough of the noise in the back seat. The dad pulled over to the curb, put the little boy on the curb, and pulled away from the boy as if he was being left behind. This made the 5 year old sister get HYSTERICAL that her brother was being left.

Then the father stopped and let the kid back in the car.

In later years the boy was threatened – and driven to the gates of – a boy's reform school, to force him to do what the parents commanded.

The little boy grew up to be a champion pre-Olympic athlete, college graduate, and political environmental activist. When he coached a kids' soccer team, he refused to keep score, so EVERYONE could feel like a winner.

He was also insecure – despite being very handsome and smart– about anyone truly loving him – and kept getting girlfriends and wives who were verbally cruel to him – the same verbal put-downs he grew up with – and was emotionally unhappy. He would "freeze" at any instance of conflict, after being hit and abused so much at home, and was skills-light in adult relationships.

# # #

EXAMPLE:

One girl's mother, dying from cancer, exacted a death-bed promise from her father that he would finish putting her through college. She was a cum laude student and was working part time jobs. The daughter discovered six weeks after her mother was buried, that her father had no intention of keeping his promise.

He ridiculed her all the time. He said she didn't need to go to college because she would just get pregnant and have to get married anyway. (She was a virgin at this time.) Then he went on to insult her that all she needed to learn how to do was clean toilets, because she'd be doing a lot of that.

She went on to be a newscaster, newspaper columnist, and author, and graduated from graduate school and post-grad classes.

She also volunteered for abused children as an investigator into their cases, when no one was standing up for them.

The way she "gave back" was to give FREE interest assessment tests to young girls who were working as waitresses and couldn't afford such career counseling "extras" – she paid for them herself and gave them to the girls – and it boosted their confidence, so that some went on to get promoted to decent jobs.

# # #

EXAMPLE:

One preteen boy had been arguing with his mother and he was verbally holding his own with her, which she then took to be a matter of "disrespect" – because she actually wanted power-over the kid. She told him to remove his belt and lean over her knees, drop his pants, and she proceeded to beat him with a belt more than a dozen times, as hard as she could. At the end of this time when she was winded and tired out, she said to him: "Have you had enough now?" And the very brave and insightful kid – just asking to be punished some more – said to her; "Have YOU had enough?" She was shocked into silence for the rest of the day and evening.

She detested her drunk husband, and referred to him when talking to the kids as "your alcoholic father" – as if he were not her "alcoholic husband!" But she tried to protect the children from his anger and put-downs as much as she could. It was just that when she was angry at the father, she took it out on this one kid, the "scapegoat" kid of the family. Because he was a defiant kid, she worried that he would become an alcoholic "bad boy" like his father – and she was trying to "discipline" it out of him. He grew up lacking in confidence, despite being an excellent athlete, and student – even after 10,000 hours of abuse.

# # #

Avoid the old cast of characters

To recover, you need to be with more supportive people.

Your recovery, and your life-long health, depends upon you hanging out with POSITIVE PEOPLE who can be HAPPY FOR YOU and for YOUR life's good moments.

It is necessary for everyone to accept the fact that there are family members – and sometimes lovers, spouses, and friends – who do not want to change at the rate you want to change – and you may have to leave them behind, which is the nature of human growth. If they want to live in the world of 4th grade, and live that over and over, that is their choice. It is a less mature life than the person who changes and grows – being stunted is to remain abnormally immature.

But know that this may be a situation you can encounter, that you must DEFEND yourself against. No one has the right, as Dr. Wayne Dwyer says; "...to take the wind out of your sails." If you – and your heart (which may be with the support of God or a higher power), are set on a new course, keep sailing.

When you make a decision, remember to check with yourself whether you are deciding out of fear, or are making the decision out of love. Someone who CANNOT BE HAPPY FOR YOU - may be acting out of FEAR that you will give them less attention. They are not acting out of LOVE for your new opportunities. Keep it in mind.

It can feel sad and painful, to leave some of these people behind, but remember, they have chosen their path. Every day, we all get a fresh chance to start over, even in tiny, tiny ways. This is why some families are so surprising when you look at them. Some of this may be due to the fact that every child arrives into a different family. At the beginning of the family's life, there may more energy available from parents, but there may not be much money. Or it might be the <u>reverse</u> situation. But the first child has an entirely different family experience than the last of multiple children. If a parent has died, the presence of a stepmother or stepfather may also have entirely changed the safety – or made there be a LACK of safety – in the family.

KEY POINTS –

- HAVE A HANDY STORY TO TELL: When you cut yourself off from your relatives or former companions, or see them infrequently, have a handy "explanation" that closes down discussion, such as: "Oh, everybody's family is a little crazy – mine's no different – but we all just live and let live." End of discussion.
- Sometimes the thought may be appealing to be an orphan – to just be clear of all the past pain and distress. If it makes it easier for you, tell folks you're an orphan, and you don't want to discuss it.
- Don't try to rescue other people, unless it's your paid job to do so. It's like the instructions on using oxygen on airplanes – give YOURSELF the oxygen first. It's too emotionally distressing for the formerly abused, who are now trying to keep living as SURVIVORS.
- You can only attempt to <u>control yourself</u>.

Grieve the past and move on to joy

Complete the grieving process, to free up your internal energy and hope. No matter where you are in the grieving process, <u>make time for joy</u>.

Psychologist Martha Beck suggests that joy is built upon several of the following things:

- Be as honest a person as you can possibly be. Lies tangle up the brain and leave us anxious – less joyful.
- Get away from and completely give up, toxic people. Some people have no interest in growing or changing and so they will not be forthcoming with love, affection or respectful treatment toward you if they have been toxic before. It's better to go find new people who will love you in a healthy way.
- Let go of bad feelings. Let the negative emotion wash over you for 90 seconds – it will pass. The bad feeling will be over soon.
- Follow your instincts. Your gut instincts can be "right" more often than a lot of mental justifications.
- Own your power. You have more strength and power than you know. Even if we fear others' reactions to doing what we want, we must defy fear, and trust that being true to ourselves, is the loving thing to do.

DUMPING GRIEF –

You will be carrying around a giant freight car of <u>painful memories</u> – baggage – negative self-image talk and lack of confidence – that will sabotage your life – <u>if you do not grieve your losses and injuries so they are dispelled</u>.

Three aspects of grieving to consider

ONE: BEING HEARTBROKEN –

Anyone who has <u>ever lost someone they loved</u>, needs to have <u>the luxury of time to weep and grieve out the pain,</u> or the heart can't cope. There is enormous loneliness that each child feels, when they feel unlovable. Grieving relieves the painful feelings, so a child's enormous burden doesn't have to keep being dragged alongside the adult. After the sadness and tears, a person can move forward to discover strengths and abilities – <u>leaving behind</u> the abusive experiences.

TWO: ANGER –

Anger, in short bursts, like fear, in short bursts, is a signal for self protection, that you need to defend yourself. Anger can also motivate a person to make changes to better themselves.

Most children who were abused can painfully remember that they could not defend themselves when they were young. They can use that memory to <u>learn and equip themselves with abilities to protect themselves</u> as adults. Others, do no change much, and some hold onto anger compulsively, because they think it will defend them. <u>Holding onto anger for a long time is not healthy</u>.

THREE: HATRED –

Anger, added to bitterness, can cause hatred. There's a limit to how long anyone can keep hatred going, because it only <u>seems</u> like strength. Hatred is really rather like a tick sucking out your blood, and depletes your energy, which is why hatred is a self-destructive emotion. Hatred also leads to violence.

For your fastest recovery: forgive to move forward, "live and let live."

Support options

Call a crisis line – there are dozens in every major metropolitan area – and they don't care if you talk about your grocery shopping list! They are funded to TAKE calls, but they are also TRAINED. It's the ideal place to anonymously spill your guts, and drop a lot of painful memories. Don't be some psychiatrist's annuity for 20 years. Dump the bad baggage – the debris left in the wound from the hurt – leave it all on the TELEPHONE HOT LINES!

You must grieve out all the painful feelings that you were storing in your body when the abuse and neglect happened, - so watch sad movies. Some good films are: "Saving Mr. Banks", "Running with Scissors", "People Like Us", "Terms of Endearment", "The Hereafter", "My Life as a Dog," Prince of Tides."

Don't sink into depression or be isolated and not ask for help, or just absorb sympathy because it's cool air on your burning wound – you must TAKE ACTION!

Listen to sad music to make you cry – you have to let tears – which carry a LOT of toxins – remove the stored adrenaline and cortisol of terror that your body has been holding, to save your health. It takes a minimum of 6 weeks to change a habit – in this case – to INTERRUPT the long-standing internal habit of ruminating of being victimized. Keep up the crying.

Hit out your grief and anger with a plastic bat on the mattress, for 6 weeks!

It's absolutely essential to find out what type of injury you sustained, so you can know how to be an advocate for others SO YOU WILL FEEL STRONGER AND A SURVIVOR AND THRIVER, instead of a victim.

Identify what TYPES of abuse you endured. Know how you reacted to the trauma. Some people, for their survival, become "pleasers" and just get re-victimized again and again. Others become OVERLY AGGRESSIVE (out of exaggerated self-protection) and become abusers of other people. Others attempt to completely NOT communicate and try to be Aspergers or schizoid in their non-contact. So overly aggressive species in nature may mate many times, but die young because of their aggression. The non-aggressive types in nature may live longer lives, but not be aggressive enough to reproduce. Know who you are, and who you want to BECOME. Take action.

Also, remember the people who DID love you. It might have been a school crossing guard, but SOMEBODY was kind to you, and just remembering it, strengthens you.

You may not have felt that you are worth much, because PETTY AND CRUEL abusers constantly did humiliating put-downs, to make you feel smaller so they would feel taller, which eroded your self esteem down to nothing. You are NOT an imposter – you DESERVE to succeed - the abuser LIED to you, making you feel bad, to evade consequences for them.

Just because you have scars, and were bleeding, and were belittled, does not mean that you failed. You SURVIVED! You were forced to give undeserved trust to an abusive adult or older sibling or cousin or neighbor – who hurt you! This did not mean YOU were WEAK – your body survived it! Your body is a HERO'S body. Scarred, but HERE.

A NIGHTLY EXERCISE –

The journal of Positive Psychology found that listing five things your are grateful for, every night before you go to bed, for a week, cures mild depression as effectively as antidepressant medications! Being grateful changes the brain's hormones and makes you more happy and content. Researchers found that one seven-day course of thanks kept people uplifted for six months.

A DAILY EXERCISE –

The following exercise is easier to do when you speak and think of yourself in the <u>third person</u> – it cuts down on the distress and causes less tears.

SAY DAILY "Forgive her/him (yourself) because you know that they suffered. Love her/him, because you've traveled together, and survived painful times. He/she (you) is a good person."

Many of us do not adequately care for or *appreciate* our bodies, because they were abused when we were little, so we felt that it was somehow the body and OUR fault that we were not strong enough to protect ourselves. Be GRATEFUL TO YOUR BODY – it helped you survive.

Every night before you go to sleep, thank your self for taking care of all the things it did that day, and thank your body for all the hard work it did carrying you around.

Know your own learning preferences and interests. Find out how you actually prefer to learn and function. If you are an introverted person – you may be able to work for an employer for hours and hours, doing high quality work – with little or no supervision. If you are an extrovert, you may be an excellent person to manage a front desk at a hotel. You need to find out what you are TRULY interested in – not keep doing what your dysfunctional family MADE you do to help them out while they were under pressure.

DOING is what causes the fastest healing. DOING comes first, followed by BEING, followed by learning different levels of appropriate TRUST, followed by LOVING.

Get a handle on what you are really like. Heal faster by getting the Strong Interest Indicator for career interests, and get MBTI testing.

There are several personality surveys you can take that will help you get a handle on what you are really like, give you good insights about your strengths and good qualities, and help you identify what to work on first. Versions of these "tests" are available free on the Web. If you wanted to take just one of them, consider taking an MBTI personality test. The version discussed here is available online at humanmetrics.com.

First, indicate YES/NO to the list of survey questions. An example is "You feel at ease in a crowd." If you can't easily answer YES or NO, for example you might feel "well, it depends on the crowd", then give the YES or NO answer that is nearest, without thinking too much about it. The test works well if you are spontaneous about it.

The survey will take less than 10 minutes. When you are done, click the SCORE It! button. It will give you a four letter code, such as "ESTJ". Don't worry too much about what the code means, just click to view the "Self-Awareness and Personal Growth" panel.

Read the description carefully. Print it and think about it, because it will have some strengths that you may be underestimating (e.g. an "ESTJ", thrives on order, focuses on family, loves to provide good service, strong work ethic, etc. An ESTJ would do well to pick a job related to production; an ESTJ is great with things, more than people or ideas).

You must decide your attitude toward your abuser(s). Come to a position of "emotional closure" in terms of how you FEEL about the person or people who abused you. Closure means you will not keep ruminating or repeating negative things to yourself mentally. Some people just adopt a position of feeling merciful and live and let live, but avoid seeing the abusers if possible.

Everyone gets hurt, it is part of life. People especially get hurt when they're young and defenseless. As an ADULT – you "chose" who you let "hurt" you!

Research has proved that the majority of abusers were themselves abused – and were told not to tell – and were told that it was their fault – and were told that it was "normal". It is possible for some people to do a "limited forgiveness" of their abusers, and just have zero future contact with them. For some people, it works to forgive, to move forward.

You want to try to have your life equation have more joy than pain, by putting out your best efforts. Your best efforts are actions! Not wishing, not hoping for rescue, not looking to be co-dependent but to take actions on your own behalf!

Actions to take to complete parenting include:

- Make yourself bully proof – in the way you wish a dad had done
- Join Toastmasters or other organizations, where you get to talk to older adults who are your parents age – and build your own family
- Join in activities that have a physical component, since research shows the scent of older males can be reassuring, and in young people, even slows down puberty.

Learn your REAL strengths and interests. And be self-loving every day.

Every day increase your self validation

Say to yourself every morning and every evening:

You are kind.

You are smart.

You are loved.

You can make mistakes.

You are valuable.

Neglect or abuse is a part of your life journey

Check for symptoms of Post Traumatic Stress Disorder to identify that neglect and/or abuse occurred, so you can integrate what happened with your present life.

PTSD Symptoms range from problems breathing, sleeping, to ringing in the ears, to forms of behavior that may seem like Aspergers or autism, or conduct disorder, or being schizoid and uncommunicative – and you may flinch at loud noises.

Give yourself credit for having SURVIVED, and know that you now can get the skills to INTEGRATE, MOURN, and REBUILD your life.

Now, as an adult, the survivors (no longer victims), can tell themselves that they are truly HEROES. Tell yourself: "You've been a hero. You've been scared. You've probably bled. You've been wounded. And you CAME THROUGH IT!"

Remember the "FACTS"

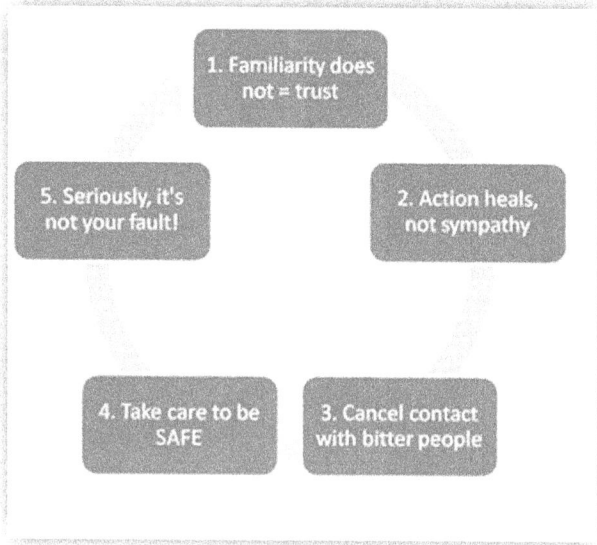

1. Familiarity does not = trust

2. Action heals, not sympathy

3. Cancel contact with bitter people

4. Take care to be SAFE

5. Seriously, it's not your fault!

IN CLOSING, KEEP THE "FACTS" IN MIND:

- Familiarity does not equal trustworthiness – trust wisely – don't give undeserved trust.
- Action heals you – take steps to do things for *you* – sympathy does not heal you.
- Cancel contact with bitter, depressed people , who drain your optimism. They're ill and need medical attention. You can not fix them – and you're not growing at the same rate.
- Take care to be safe at all times – you come first – stop rescuing people – they need to grow.
- Seriously, it's not your fault!

Author's Bio

Ann Ford

Ford has a M.S. in counseling psychology, Phi Kappa Phi, and did post-graduate work and instructed at Johns Hopkins in adult learning styles. She has counseled over 300 clients, primarily as part of large business downsizings, helping people through grief, forced change, and how to start over. She has lectured to university psychology departments on the cycle of domestic violence, taught court-ordered DV offenders new skills and taught the domestic violence cycle to incoming police recruits, and has conducted seminars nationally on sexual harassment.

She's been published in many publications, has been a columnist, and in recent years has won a few literary awards, writing books on multiple subjects, including a children's book on Hiroshima.

She's been nominated for a broadcasting award from American Women in Radio and Television, and won a Communications Arts Award, for work in her first career, which was radio and television broadcasting.

Bibliography

Ann Ford, in her books "**Big Hot Mess Borderlines**" and "**If a Borderline Loves You**", deals with family and love relationships with borderlines and other difficult people.

Dr. Charles Whitfield specializes in helping victims of childhood trauma. His books include "*Healing the Child Within*", "*Memory and Abuse*", and "*The Truth About Mental Illness*".

The *Diagnostic and Statistical Manual of Mental Disorders* (DSM) specifies diagnostic and statistical data for doctors.

One of the best books on trauma, titled "**Trauma**" by Judith Herman, Ph.D., covers the *damage done to people* in war, domestic traumas, and rape traumas.

Olivier Ameisen claimed in his book *The Last Glass* that he had cured himself of alcoholism by treating himself with high doses of the drug baclofen.

Psychology Today is a general interest magazine that covers the range of human behavior.

Index

abusers...6, 7, 9, 10, 14, 16, 22, 23, 31, 36, 38, 45, 57, 63, 80, 122, 137, 140

Alateen 126

alcoholic 24, 32, 39, 40, 55, 56, 57, 67, 75, 87, 89, 91, 93, 96, 99, 102, 103, 106, 129, 131

Angelina Jolie............................ 55

anti-depressants 31, 73

Ariel Winter 8

Aspergers 44, 45, 63, 137, 142

B vitamins 60

B12 shots.................................. 47

Berlin Wall............................... 26

Beth Israel Hospital.................. 16

Beyonce Knowles........................ 7

Brryan Jackson 21

bullying 30, 31, 32, 46

Catholic 11, 12, 70, 98

Catholic church 11

Charles Whitfield 123, 146

child abuse.... 5, 6, 7, 9, 11, 13, 14, 15, 16, 19, 21, 38, 62, 67, 95, 97, 102, 106, 114, 118, 123, 126

Christian Brothers 12

coach 6, 11, 14, 20, 35

college ...12, 35, 36, 40, 69, 70, 73, 83, 84, 93, 94, 103, 109, 129, 130

crime 5, 22

cruelty....26, 27, 28, 29, 38, 43, 45, 91

Darlene Jo Lewis........................ 7

domestic violence6, 39, 48, 67, 96, 98, 101, 102, 107, 121, 126, 145

dopamine............................ 37, 60

Dr. Phil.................................... 10

drinking. 16, 17, 24, 25, 38, 39, 40, 41, 73, 83, 89, 92, 94, 99, 103, 111

drug abuse............................ 19, 38

drugs 16, 19, 21, 28, 30, 37, 38, 41, 45, 80, 81

DSM-IV.................................... 25

Edward Courtney 11

EFT............................. 60, 126, 128

EMDR 60, 126, 128

Emotional Freedom Technique. 60, 126

Erica Susan Perdue 13

forgiveness......................... 51, 119

GABA......................... 37, 39, 111

Heather Orr 118

homeless 7

hormone.................. 27, 37, 38, 60

impulsiveness............................ 28

jail. 5, 6, 12, 13, 22, 50, 51, 81, 88, 118

Jon Hamm........................... 10, 15

Jon Voight 55

Josh Powell............................. 101

Joyful Heart Foundation 6

Judith Herman, Ph.D..........45, 146

Julia Roberts 6

Kristen Breitweiser 128

Lindsey Lowe 12

love 23, 28, 29, 138

Macaulay Culkin..................... 127

Mackenzie Phillips.................. 120

Maya Angelou 43

MBTI 139

Megan Huntsman...................... 21

mental disorders........................ 25

mentally ill.... 7, 18, 21, 22, 23, 44, 49, 50, 114

Mike Tyson............................... 35

money..6, 7, 17, 50, 82, 84, 85, 91, 92, 93, 96, 97, 98, 102, 103, 105, 108, 115, 126, 127, 133

Munchausen's By Proxy 19

narcissist 24, 26

neglect 9, 16, 17, 18, 23, 26, 38, 44, 49, 50, 55, 62, 63, 95, 118, 122, 123, 124, 126, 128, 136, 142

Newtown, CT 29

nudity 6

Olivier Ameisen 37

Oprah Winfrey 14, 125, 126

Post Traumatic Stress Disorder 44, 53, 54, 62, 89, 111, 116, 122, 142

POWs 32

predator 26, 27

PTSD 44, 48, 62, 63, 122, 142

rage 24, 30, 31, 51, 76, 92, 93, 114

rapists 36

Sandusky 6

Seattle Archdiocese 12

serotonin 60

shame 6, 64, 126

step-parents 17

stigma 6

Strong Interest Indicator 139

Sugar Ray Leonard 35

survivors 9

testosterone 27, 35, 38

victim 9, 11, 39, 45, 46, 57, 125, 136

Walt Disney 14

William Glasser, M.D. 27

zinc 60

www.ingramcontent.com/pod-product-compliance
Lightning Source LLC
Chambersburg PA
CBHW072017040426

42447CB00009B/1654